BEAGLE TALES 3

BY

BOB FORD

ILLUSTRATED BY

ALEXIS MORRISON

BEAGLE TALES 3

FIRST SUNBURY PRESS EDITION
Printed in the United States of America
November 2012

Trade Paperback ISBN: 978-1-62006-140-4
Mobipocket format (Kindle) ISBN: 978-1-62006-141-1
ePub format (Nook) ISBN: 978-1-62006-142-8

Published by:
Sunbury Press
Mechanicsburg, PA
www.sunburypress.com

Mechanicsburg, Pennsylvania   USA

From The American Beagler

We were contacted by the publisher of **Beagle Tales**, by Bob Ford about advertising the book in our magazine, *The American Beagler*. Of course, we were interested in running an ad and also requested a copy of the book. After reading the book we contacted Sunbury Press with a message for Bob Ford to contact us to see about the possibility of having him write a monthly article in *The American Beagler*.

We were thrilled when Bob gave us the opportunity to feature him as a writer. We were excited to get a writer of his caliber for a monthly article. We take copies of *Beagle Tales* and the latest issues of *The American Beagler Magazine* with Bob's articles to the Beagle Hunts. We find people laughing and reading the articles out loud.

We are looking forward to Bob's next book.

The American Beagler Magazine
Mike and Janie Ridenhour
PO Box 957
Belle, MO 65013
573-859-6866
www.theamericanbeagler.com
ridenhour000@centurytel.net

From
Hounds and Hunting

We are very pleased to be able to include Bob's writing in *Hounds and Hunting*. His articles bring a fresh, fun approach to the love of beagling.

Our staff anticipates a chuckle with each article, and he never disappoints.

Hounds and Hunting
Since 1903
The Only Magazine Featuring All Types of
Beagle Field Trials
www.houndsandhunting.com

Acknowledgments

This book is dedicated to the hounds, past and present, who have given me so many good hours afield. I would like to thank The American Beagler and Hounds and Hunting, both of these magazines feature my writing. I also offer great appreciation to the Bellwood Beagle Club--It is good to have so many wonderful brothers in beagling. As always, my wife is deserving of special credit--she has tolerated more than she anticipated when she married a beagle-running, rabbit-hunting preacher.

"But when they are really close to the hare they will make the matter plain to the huntsman by various signs—the quivering of their bodies backwards and forwards, sterns and all; the ardour meaning business; the rush and emulaton; the hurry-scurry to be first; the patient following-up of the whole pack; at one moment massed together, and at another separated; and once again the steady onward rush. At last they have reached the hare's form, and are in the act to spring upon her. But she on a sudden will start up and bring about her ears the barking clamour of the whole pack as she makes off full speed. Then as the chase grows hot, the view halloo! of the huntsman may be heard: "So ho, good hounds! that's she! cleverly now, good hounds! so ho, good hounds!" And so, wrapping his cloak about his left arm, and snatching up his club, he joins the hounds in the race after the hare, taking care not to get in their way, which would stop proceedings. The hare, once off, is quickly out of sight of her pursuers; but, as a rule, will make a circuit back to the place where she was found."

--Xenophon, Cynegeticus, BK VI, 4th century B.C., describing hounds that may be the ancestors of beagles.

7 ¶O 3

Spring has sprung. Not that we had much of a winter. Sure, I know that plenty of people are happy. I have a whiskey barrel that I bought from *Lowes* as a planter, and it is bulging with chives. I grow them inside the barrel for fear that they would get mowed in the early season. I worry about this potentiality because on several occasions as a kid I mowed my father's chives. Finally, after several attempts to replace them, dad placed his chives near the pussy willow bush and told me not to mow anywhere near that—he would tend that area. Young chives did not look very distinct whenever I mowed them, although I could smell my error after the fact. Then, another year, my younger sister picked the chives after they blossomed and gave them to mom saying, "Here mommy, they are pretty purple flowers but they stink a little." I believe we ate a stew containing large amounts of chives for supper that night. The only other flowers we ever gave mom were dandelions and buttercups. Well, I once picked the neighbors tulips, but that is another story. Her Mother's Day gifts were either homemade or utilitarian—cooking utensils and such. Once I got her an answering machine with my hard earned money, but that was selfish—I wanted to know if any girls called while no one was home. They never did, incidentally.

Moms often get left out of beagling achievements. Sure, there are plenty of gals that field trial and hunt, but there are even more that, shall we say, tolerate their husband's beagle passions. When I say tolerate I mean do a lot of work. When I was a kid Dad or I fed the dogs each night. But there were occasions when neither of us was home at dusk, especially in the summer. Changing shifts each week was a part of reality for my father, who worked at a factory, and often was earning his income at feeding time.

There were all sorts of oddities about changing shifts. For instance, if Dad worked from 3 to 11 then mom made a big dinner at noon and the leftovers went into the refrigerator for supper after school was out for the day. She ate the same meal twice. If my father worked 7 to 3 there was no elaborate lunch in the event that it was not a school day— you made a sandwich or something. Those days she cooked supper. She wasn't cooking two meals unless dad was off work that day. The 3 to 11 shift was nice for us kids. We could make noise. When Dad worked 11 o 7 he would be trying to sleep in the day and we had to tiptoe and whisper. Nothing was worse than trying to have an argument with your sister while whispering.

"I told you no. That candy bar is mine," I would whisper while making the facial expressions that typically accompanies shouting.

"You don't even like *Three Musketeers*, you are just saving it cuz you know I like them," my sister explained with her teeth clenched shut, as if that made her voice more quiet.

"So what. That doesn't matter. If you go buy a *Snickers* I will trade you," I raised my voice to a normal talking volume, signifying that the fight was over, as far as I was concerned. Later the candy bar would be gone, the empty wrapper as missing as Jimmy Hoffa, leaving no evidence. I would then start taking random items that belonged to my sister as war reparations. She would begin to argue with me in a whisper, but soon her vocal range entered that register best described as "squeaky, high-pitched sister scream." She had one higher note that she would hit when she was real mad, but she appeared mute and it evoked no sympathy, it merely set all the dogs in a 3 mile radius howling.

BOOM! The door to mom and dad's room opened and slammed shut. Dad started down the stairs. I grabbed a comic book and sat on the couch, reading the book as if I were studying for a major exam. Sis ran to the chair and pretended to be napping.

"What the hell is going on here, don't you know I gotta work tonight?" Dad glared at us.

2

"What's that dad?" sis yawned, "I was trying to sleep too." I looked at her in disbelief.

Dad fixed his gaze on me, "If I come back down here, you're in for it," he said.

"Why me? Why not her?" I pleaded.

"Cuz," he said, "You're the instigator, even when she is in the wrong," and he trudged back upstairs.

Whenever dad worked 3 to 11 we could really shout. But as we got older we were never home in the evening, especially in the summer. I never even wondered how the beagles would get fed, mom just did it. Who kept track of shots, vaccinations and AKC paperwork? Mom. I do not recall ever buying a bag of dog food. Sure, I would carry the 50 pound bag into the house, but she had to load it into the car. This was back when they sold 50 pound bags, before they removed 6 pounds and raised the price. If memory serves me correctly I think I even remember 55 pound bags once upon a time. Mom could wrestle those big bags too. When it comes to pound for pound strength there are legendary animals like weasels and ants. Working class, rural moms are right up there too.

Hey, while we are talking about motherly contributions to our sport, let's be honest about something else: most of the food we ever ate at a beagle club that tasted good was cooked by a mother. Sure, as men we sometimes handle breakfast at the field trials while mom is at home getting all the kids awake and ready to go to the clubhouse, but most club kitchens are not as efficient when the women are not around. Anxiety abounds if someone asks for eggs in any fashion other than over easy.

"Can I get my eggs scrambled on top of my potatoes?" a field trialer might request.

The guy taking the money stares at the handler and says, "You can have dippy eggs."

This isn't to say that there aren't some men that know their way around the kitchen. I have been to clubs where some guy that owns a restaurant caters the food for his own club. At that point the rest of the members serve as his kitchen staff and the food is good. But, nine times out of ten, an all male kitchen does not produce as good of a product—unless the food was cooked at home by somebody's wife and brought to the trial requiring nothing more than a little "warming up." Soups, stews, casseroles, and desserts can all be made at home. With some training we men can be taught to transport the vittles to the club and heat them up. Baked beans with lots of meat and a variety of variously shaped beans are indicative of a woman's touch. Lots of one type of bean in a bowl is a good sign that I stopped at the store and bought a can that said "baked beans" on the label. If you are eating with real utensils instead of a plastic fork that doesn't have quite enough tensile strength to power through the meatloaf, then women must be in the clubhouse somewhere. If the men folk have the clubhouse duties we use plastic and throw them out.

Mothers are essential to our beagling endeavors. At the age of sixteen I was legally permitted to hunt alone. My parents would often give me permission to miss a day of school here and there—with good grades being prerequisite. Sometimes, however, the urge to hunt would be overpowering and I would not be able to contain myself. I would ditch school without parental permission. The teacher would be rambling on about equations, quotients, integers and formulas and the only number I could think about was 4—the daily limit of rabbits. This was especially true in the early season. The trees would be golden and auburn in their foliage, how was I supposed to think about parabolas and variables?

So, on occasion, I would sneak out of the building and go home. This was possible only when dad was on a 7 to 3 shift and mom was on an all day errand. There were lots of four rabbit weekday sorties in November. My favorite hooky hunt happened on a cold day when the frost hung on the ground until mid-morning. I had a bad case of rabbit fever that developed when I got to school and saw the blue sky getting bright. When the bell rang signifying the end of homeroom I went to the restroom and waited. There would be three minutes of rapid movement in the hallway as students walked to first period. The halls echoed with hundreds of voices that blended into a deafening din that had no discernible words. It sounded like a loud version of Charlie Brown's teacher, but with an

4

echo. Then a bell followed by silence. I waited a few long minutes and bolted out of the building and ran for home!

I scrambled into the house (remember when no one locked doors?) and put on my hunting clothes and grabbed dad's shotgun. Hey, if you are going to be bad, you may as well go all the way. Plus, Dad had a better gun! I leashed the dogs and started running with them. It was another mile to good rabbit cover, and I had to go through terrific deer habitat to get there—no sense unleashing the dogs and risking a blissful hunt descending into a trash run. The oaks and mountain laurel gave way to early growth birch and then goldenrod. I unleashed the dogs and sat to catch my breath. By the time my heart rate and respiration calmed the two dogs had found a rabbit. It was great! I missed a few rabbits that holed, providing a downtrodden feeling. This only made the thrill of shooting a rabbit feel even better! I shot my third rabbit on a big running rabbit that made several circles before I ever saw it and several more before I was able to shoot at it. I missed and the cottontail relocated in the next valley, where I was able to sneak in on the chase and intercept him for the kill. It was getting warm as the sun climbed and the dogs were panting. I felt a little bad that I missed several rabbits and would not get my limit, but I was elated over the great morning. The tired dogs and I walked home at a much slower pace, pausing at a creek and later a mud puddle for the beagles to rehydrate. The back of my game vest was heavy with bunnies and a bonus woodcock that the hounds flushed while chasing a rabbit. It flew right at me. The front pockets of my vest were full of apples that that were a bit tart, but looked almost store bought, minus the wax that grocers apply.

All of this was accomplished by 1:00 p.m. Now came the critical part of the ruse. I had to clean the rabbits (and the bird) and get them frozen. Hooky hunting did not permit the soaking of bunnies in salt water--how would I explain a pot of meat in the refrigerator? If, however, I froze them immediately after rinsing and put the meat into the freezer with the other wild game, there was no way to know when the critters were taken. Pretty slick, huh? All that was left was to put on the exact same clothes that I was wearing when I left the house for school and go hide for a little bit before walking into the house about 3:00. I took the apples with me, stuffed into my book bag, when I evacuated the house before the return of my mother, who was gone all day taking her mother to the doctor. I sat by a stream and read one of Jack London's books from my backpack for a book report. I forget if it was *White Fang* or *Call of the Wild*. I did do some school work after all.

I walked into the door and heaved my shoulders with a sigh to convey the difficulty of the day. I plopped my book bag on the chair as I always did and pulled out the apples and washed them for the fruit bowl, eating the last one rinsed. Mom was whipping up supper for Dad. It was a 7 to 3 day, after all.

"Nice looking apples," mom said.

"Yeah, I figured why let 'em rot. I got 'em on the way home."

Imagine my surprise when dad walked in the door and said "If we hurry we may have time to get a couple bunnies." I hurriedly got dressed and dad opted to hit the brush in his work clothes, just adding his hunting vest and an orange hat. Of course there wasn't much time, but a little bit. So we had to hunt close. Real close, about one mile from home. The same spot I had just hunted.

"The dogs aren't finding too much," Dad said, puffing his pipe.

Finally they jumped a good rabbit and the chase was on. Dad tumbled the bunny after the first circle. When he walked over to the dead rabbit he almost stepped on another cottontail and it burst out into the open. "Tally-Ho!" he yelled. The dogs were already there as they were coming hard on the scent of the dead rabbit. The sun transitioned from being in my eyes to mostly behind the western hills allowing me to finally look west without squinting. I saw the rabbit running straight at me, a shot that I am still known for missing. I slowly squeezed the trigger when I gauged the distance to be close enough to hit but far enough away for a good spread. And there, fifteen yards in front of me, lay my fourth rabbit of the day.

"Must be hotter than it feels," Dad said, "those dogs look awful tired for all the more they ran. I was sure dad was on to me, but he wasn't.

We headed for home with a bit of twilight left and ate supper before cleaning the two rabbits. By the way, supper included hot apple pie from my morning scavenging. It was still a bit too hot to eat, but nothing a few scoops of vanilla ice cream couldn't solve. We cleaned the rabbits and soaked them in the cellar refrigerator, an old appliance that dad found at a yard sale and cobbled together. It mostly held game, fishing bait, and dad's beer. Sometimes a frozen turkey might gradual thaw in there, so long as there was no fishing bait that might surprise mom. She was fine with dead mammals, just not worms. The bunnies were placed in cook pot to soak on the top shelf. It was the perfect day of hooky.

I woke up the next morning and mom met me at the door with lunch money and a kiss on the forehead.

"Oh, here," she said handing me a slip of paper.

I read it. It said, "Please excuse Robert Ford from school yesterday, he had a fever."

"What's this," I said.

"The school left a message on that answering machine you bought me last year. It said that you were not absent when attendance was taken during home room, but no teacher saw you all day."

I blinked at her in disbelief. This was not my first round of hooky, how did I get caught? "I-I-I, umm," I stammered.

"You're math teacher returned your tests and you weren't in class, even though you were in school," mom said.

I was caught by the daily announcement sheet. It was a single sheet of paper delivered during first period by some apple polishing kid that the teachers liked. Somebody different did it each day. When the sheet arrived into the classroom it smelled like fresh ink—from the ditto machine, this was before modern photocopiers. The page listed absences as well as those to be excused early, and any special events.

"I called the school office already," Mom said, "I told them that your homeroom teacher must have had you listed as present when you were really absent."

"Really?" I was shocked at her pleasing tone.

"I was gonna write that you had rabbit fever, but I didn't. Just don't have any bad grades when that report card arrives.

Happy Mother's Day everyone. Be careful what you buy mom. Get her something that has no practical value whatsoever, something extravagant. Definitely don't get her an answering machine.

BASS VERSUS RABBITS

My wife hails from the Adirondacks, and we sometimes venture north to see her family (the in-laws). My family is mostly here in Pennsylvania (the outlaws) and we have opportunity to see them a bit more frequently, although we really don't take advantage of that option due to the fact that kids are too busy. If you ever want to see what I am talking about, just go visit a relative with a bunch of kids and look at the refrigerator. Start by looking inside. The damn things will look like mother Hubbard's cupboard, because the kids begin training in soccer, T-ball, gymnastics, dance, acting, tennis, and "play dates" before they can even walk.

A play date, for the uninitiated, is when parents schedule a time for the kids to play with somebody else's kids. Such a monstrous invention is required due to the hectic schedule that said children maintain, ensuring that they have no free time. The goal, as far as I can tell, is to generate children who can list at least a dozen extracurricular activities on their college applications to give them the edge over other children applying to the same school. The sacrifice for all those activities is basic education. Ever tried to get a teenager who is working the cash register to ring up your sale manually under a power outage? They can't make change. What is even more difficult is giving a teenager a twenty dollar bill and a penny to pay for a purchase totaling $1.26. Such a purchase just happened to me at a convenience store.

"Uhh, Dude," the girl said "Like the Penny is totally more than like you like need to like pay for this bottle of water. Like, you know what I mean? Like, you already have a twenty dollar bill here." It is important for them to say the word "like" as often as they can.

"I know," I answered, "I was just trying to get eighteen dollars and three quarters for change rather than the 74 cents." I could see the gears turning in her head, and knew that she could not comprehend what I was saying.

"I don't know how to, like, do that, so like, I am going to like give you the penny back and like run it through the register." She said.

"O.K."

"$18.74 is your change," she said, omitting the word "like" because it was not written on the cash register, which is where she read the amount of change that I was to be given.

"Here," I said while giving her the 74 cents and adding a penny, "Could I get three quarters?"

"Gee, like thanks Mister!" She said, "I was like totally getting low on pennies." No doubt her list of extracurricular activities is stellar. But I digress.

If, after looking into the bare fridge in the home full of kids, you then look at the actual exterior of the fridge door, the sight will shock you. The door will be covered with calendars. Each child will have his or her own calendar that details the monthly cycle of practices, meetings, tournaments, and games. In many instances there will also be a master calendar. This will be for the parents who try desperately to coordinate all the transportation that will be required to get their kids into an Ivy League school. There will also be coupons for pizza parlors, hoagie shops, and other eateries. The end product is a refrigerator door that looks more complicated than an engineer's little book of complex math formulas—the math that is full of symbols rather than numbers. The coupons are to feed the child. Mom will pick the kid up from soccer practice and shove a burger down his throat as they travel to piano lessons. This is why there is very little food in the house—no one is home. It is also why salesmen seem to think that cup holders are a feature that people find important when selecting a vehicle. Don't bother asking a car salesman about horsepower, torque, or gear ratios in the differentials. These are alien concepts to today's peddlers of horseless carriages. Rather, they specialize in cup holders that prevent children from spilling, and little television screens to entertain them as you drive down the road—heaven forbid they be forced to interact with other humans in the vehicle, or invent a traveling game with their imaginations.

So, I do manage to see my outlaws a bit, but we take one or two extended trips to the Adirondacks to see my wife's kin each year. My father-in-law drives tractor trailer, and he parks his rig on a farm several miles from his home that is excellent cover for hare. He also owns land near the Saranac river and we camp there in the late summer or early fall to avoid the Pennsylvania heat and humidity. My wife says that her dad is planning on letting her have the land really soon, and that we may be able to build a little shack for our stays, rather than use tents as we do now. I knew this land existed before we got married—hey there is only an "n" that differentiates fiancé from finance! A good marriage can finance a camp in the mountains near a world class trout river. But bass are all the rage in the nearby town of Plattsburgh, which sits along Lake Champlain. We have been there during the big bass tournament.

Now, I have only recently been permitted to eat fish. It seems I had an incident as a kid while eating fish, and I was diagnosed as allergic. By incident, I mean my face swelled and I quit breathing. I had the same reaction to eggs as a toddler. So, when I was kid fish was not on the menu. I was permitted to thaw some venison for supper whilst everyone else ate seafood. Then, as I approached the age of 40 my physician felt I should get the flu vaccine, especially since a large part of my workday is spent in hospitals or nursing homes with sick people. An egg allergy precluded the vaccine because the flu vaccine is made with eggs. Not to be deterred, the Doc sent me for testing. Apparently I am no longer allergic to eggs or seafood. Although I was told as a kid that I could probably eat freshwater fish, I never did take the chance. So I now get a weak flu every year (the first two days after I get the vaccine) and I can eat things that I never have tried before.

Having not eaten fish for my whole life, I can say this: I wasn't missing much. Trout I like. Some pan fish are good. Most of it is not appealing to me, including bass, which must be why they are always released after being caught. Whenever I watch the television programs about hunting and fishing there are always people talking about how delicious venison, pheasant, duck, and elk taste, and there is very often a little bit of filler material after they hunt where the master hunter is filmed as a master chef on the grill. They almost never cook inside.

What they should do is have the fishing shows end with the master angler cooking on the grill. "Well." A guy with a soothing Southern accent would say. "I started my journey to become a professional fisherman by watching Orlando Wilson as a kid—and here I am today showing you how to cook your catch! Now, always cook this stuff outside, cuz you can't never get the stench of cooked bass out of your house..."

And that would be honest, at least for me. I'd say the same for catfish. We beaglers, by contrast, pursue one of the most delicious game species anywhere. Which makes me think of that bass tournament in Plattsburgh—why do they make so much money catching bass and no one is getting rich training beagles and hunting rabbits? Sure, there are guys hunting deer on TV, but very little attention is given to any small game other than winged. I especially like the whitetail shows where the host feigns being surprised to see a deer. If you look carefully you can sometimes see the trail of hay that the monster buck is following through the snow—editing never catches everything. I know that there are real hunts with real hunters at real locations on the television as well, but...

The poor beagle is looked down upon by many upland bird hunters sporting Italian over/under shotguns and pointing dogs named Winslow or Troy. Pheasant, grouse, woodcock, and other birds are great, but I don't understand the neglect of out faithful hound in the eyes of the armchair hunter. Let's face it, many people who claim to hunt really just watch hunting shows and hunt the rifle deer season. Maybe they hit the fields in pursuit of a spring gobbler, which is classified as big game in my home state. The money is clearly going to non-beagling pursuits, and those bass guys are really perplexing to me.

Have you seen the elite bass fishermen travelling? They tow fantastically expensive bass boats, (capable of kicking up a rooster tail) behind massive diesel pickup trucks big enough to sleep in--if need be. They have more patches on their shirt than a NASCAR driver and more sponsors too! Not once have I seen one of those guys driving a jalopy that barely starts. Nor have I seen one with a canoe in the bed of the truck or a big 'ol pontoon boat in tow. Granted, they are the elite bass fishermen, but the elites of beagling may not find that their efforts have been as lucrative as they might have hoped, in comparison.

To begin with, too many people think that a little alphabet soup in front of the dogs name (each registry has its own title and abbreviation for a champ) will generate enough stud money for the whole family to quit their jobs. I once knew a guy who got a win at a trial with a male dog and quit his job to find more time to train dogs and trial them in pursuit of the title of field champion. The plan was to get the three wins and 120 points required by AKC and then retire as every bitch in heat from the surrounding states was trotted over to his kennel to receive the genetic material needed whelp champion pups. Reality, it seems, is a bit different. Many of the successful field trialers I know are recently retired with a decent pension. They are able to live modestly on the road, and are still healthy enough to pursue ribbons and trophies. For the most part, however, beaglers do not arrive at competitions with the newest diesel engine to come off the Cummins factory line.

I have seen trucks with beds that rattle in the wind as the field trialer goes down the road. Primer paint is good enough (I am thinking of a jalopy that sits at my house) and the upholstery often smells like wet dog. Where a bass fisherman might be hauling a boat and trailer worth thousands, a simple wooden box in the bed is what keeps Fido the beagle contained until the field trial or hunt begins. Sponsorships are not common and no one feels a need to endorse product at the end of a hard fought day afield. There are no television reporters for our sport. What would a trial winner say?

"Well, 'Ol Rover here got it done today. I'd like to thank *Power Kibbles* brand dog food for making him tough and keeping' his turds small at the same time. Special thanks to my tracking collar manufacturer, cuz half the time I can't find the dog without it. That there dog box was built by my brother-in-law. He can make you one too."

Hey, some clubs have rabbit hunts during the season as a fundraiser where a hunter (or hunters) competes to see who can get the heaviest, lightest, or most rabbits. Still, there are no big television shows or corporate sponsors in rabbit hunting. And the rabbit is infinitely tastier than the bass. Shotgun companies and ammunition makers should be flocking to rabbit tournaments. Dog food companies and crate builders too. Makers of hunting clothes might try to woo the best rabbit hunters and the owners of the best beagles. Beaglers could travel the tournament circuit, starting in states with no closed season for some late summer tournaments. Next we would head to the states with earlier starts to the hunting season for snowshoe hare. This would be followed by days of cottontail hunts. As the weather cooled the gang would head into the southern states for those big swamp rabbits. Perhaps some western states for jackrabbits too. I would be one of the lesser guys—you know, like the guys in NASCAR that always wreck early. I can hear my interview now. I would always say something like, "We got a few rabbits after the dogs stopped sniffing each other and fighting over the stick. That deer chase in the middle screwed me up, but I found the dogs by lunchtime with my tracking collar. The dogs were too wore out to do much after that. I haven't been able to train them too much cuz it takes so long to get the tournament." I would proudly name my sponsors. And then cook the rabbits, which are way better than any bass.

THE BEAGLE WHISPERER

Ever since I was a kid, beagles have found me irresistible. I remember this happening with the neighbor's dog, his name was Whiskers. Whiskers belonged to the Dublers, a retired couple close to home. I was always at their house visiting the dog, a sort of Dennis the Menace figure for John Dubler. Whiskers spent the summers chained in the yard and roaming his owner's porch. The dog chased rabbits while John picked berries, and spent the rest of his time hunting attention in the yard. I, of course, spoiled Whiskers by letting him on the porch furniture while I groomed his shedding hair with my hands and snuck him some table scraps from my house. I always did my best to get him as much of my cube steak as possible.

I would much rather eat ground burger than cube steak. To the best of my knowledge, cube steak is made by running scraps of meat through a contraption that mashes it into a larger, steak-like shape. By steak-like I mean nothing like steak, but rather a sinewy blend of protein with multiple bands of muscle grain. Not the best cut of meat. We seemed to eat it fairly often in my home. One of my Church member's Howard Moyer, tells me that it can be made into a very tender and delicious selection—if the meat cutter isn't lazy. This was a topic of conversation with Howard and me one time. I knew I started off the conversation wrong when I mentioned my dislike of cube steak.

"I ate it a lot as a kid, and would have preferred a bowl of cereal," I squinted my left eye as I recalled the amount of time it took to chew cube steak into a piece small enough to swallow."

"I don't know why people say that," Howard corrected my assessment "If it's done right it is one of my favorite steaks." It should be noted that Howard started at the bottom of the employee chain in a grocery store and worked his way to the top, eventually managing stores and owning them. In between he held every job you could do in a grocery store, which is why I now call butchers by the title meat cutter, which is the accurate term for those who work in the business. He then explained the process I mentioned above, about the machine used to make cube steak. "The key," he said, "Is to run the meat through the blades several times in different directions. If you just run it through enough to hold it together, it will be tough."

"Evidently my mother bought her cube steak from a butcher that used a ball peen hammer," I said. Howard laughed and shook his head to imply that he had seen a few people make the steaks improperly in the past.

At any rate, when I was a kid I had developed an ingenious plan for disposing of my cube steak. First, I always took the smallest piece available. Secondly, I did eat some of the steak. I always made sure that someone saw me eating it. Usually there was a bite or two that could be processed. Lastly, I made use of my napkin, which sat on my lap. I filled my napkin with hunks of gristle and sinew. Then I transferred those bits to my pocket, which had been lined with plastic wrap.

This was my third method for disposing of cube steak and it worked pretty well. My original plan had been to scrunch it under my plate, hence presenting an "empty plate" or the prerequisite for being allowed to go outside and play. That strategy failed whenever mom put the plate in the sink to soak and she found cube steak floating in the dishwater as it fell away from the plate's bottom surface. My second plan was to place the meat in my napkin and leave it wrapped in suck a fashion until I threw it away after supper. This too failed, as she could see that my paper napkin was way too big when I was done eating.

But putting meat in my pocket worked great. My pockets were always bulging with rocks and toy cars and whatever oddities I found. At first I just took the meat outside and got rid of it. And then I remembered whiskers! I would sneak the meat over to the porch. "Here boy!" I would call him, as I fed the gnarly beef chunks to the dog."

"Boy that's a lot of meat," John would say, "Does your dad know you are giving all that to my dog?"

"Yep!" I lied.

"Really?" John gave me that look that he would hold on a person until they caved under the weight of it.

"O.K, no he doesn't." I stared at me shoe in disgust with myself, "But I don't like cube steak and I can't leave the table until it is gone."

John smiled down at me, "Well, you shouldn't do that, but I don't want to be a snitch. Just don't feed Whiskers any table food other than cube steak." From then on, Whiskers and I had a better friendship. He looked forward to seeing me in the evenings, especially on cube steak nights.

And it has been other beagles too that have loved me. My childhood friend John Zimmerman had a dog named Trapper. Trapper and I were great friends. John and I took that long-legged beagle in the woods behind his house every day in the summer. My twin nephews had a Red and white beagle with the most creative name I ever saw for a beagle with the atypical red and white coloration. They called him Red. Before I had my own beagles I was constantly bothering my nephews (6 years older than me) to take me to the woods with Red. Kim and Keith were always good about tolerating my requests, and the first varying hare I ever shot was in front of Red. Red and I were buddies, and after I got two beagles of my own he would often be the old voice of experience in our trio of rabbit running hounds. Beagles just love me.

You see, if I go into a house where a beagle is not allowed on the couch, the beast will jump right up on the couch next to me. Before you know it, the hound is up there all the time, even knowing full well that it isn't permitted on the furniture. I get the blame. My defense is that I do my best relaxing in a recliner with a beagle perched behind my head on the back of the chair. It makes more sense to have the beagle on the furniture. I tell this to the beagles as I scratch their ears saying, "Get up her beside me, it is much easier to rub your ears and check you for briars and ticks up here than to have me crawling on the floor with you." The beagle responds by thumping his tail against the upholstery and rolling onto his back to get a belly scratch. Besides, a soft cushion works great to support the bones of a hound after a long morning chase.

Once I "dog sat" (kinda like baby sitting) a hound named Sadie for a family. Sadie was a house beagle that did not chase rabbits. She played great with my beagles, and I decided to take her with me to the beagle club. Sadie followed my dogs for an hour and then started to give "me-too" barks behind the pack. The next day I took her out with just one dog and she jumped the rabbit with a sight chase, all at the age of three. I guess she still isn't the best rabbit dog, but that is because her owners do not want her to chase rabbits. I hear she is getting better at it, and is very difficult to control in her local dog park, which is full of rabbits. I have never been asked to dog sit Sadie again. I really think that Sadie is happier, and that some deep corner of her soul has been revived by the song of pursuit. I see lots of beagles that have been bred for purposes other than hunting, only to discover that the dogs still want to hunt. Oh sure, the last rabbit chasing ancestor may be so far back in the pedigree that the beagle neither tongues on a trail nor knows that a rabbit is the scent of choice, but the urges are there.

Whenever we have company stay overnight, they are in for a wild morning. My beagles have been conditioned to get up about an hour before dawn. That is the hour that I usually leave the house for the woods, and I can honestly say that I haven't required an alarm clock in so long that I do not remember the last time I awoke to one. At that early part of the day the hounds go to the woods for an hour or two before work. If I do not go, due to weather or work, then they get a big breakfast followed by a trip into the fenced yard while I have coffee. I guess some overnight company doesn't consider 5:00 a.m. a good time to hear beagles barking, did you know that? It is probably because they stay up too late watching television. How can you run dogs early if you are up till midnight? "You can't crow with the roosters and hoot with the owls" my dad was fond of saying. There isn't much worth watching on that TV anyway. Although one time we had overnight company and rented a movie from the store (boy that goes back awhile, huh?) and we watched a movie called "The Horse Whisperer." I believe the premise was about a guy that could communicate with horses so easily that it looked as if no communication was occurring at all.

This, of course, has led to a program that another parishioner showed me called "The Dog Whisperer." It is about a guy who goes into homes and gets the dogs to behave properly. I think I am able to do this with beagles. I put my forehead against theirs and pet the dog. I am communicating at a gut level with the hound. If you ever see me doing this, you may be wondering just what communication is happening. It happens in my house frequently. I will tell you my thoughts, the very ones that I send to my beagles so that you can do the same with your hounds:

"You are a beagle. Every other breed is just a dog. Sit here on my lap while I while I pet the shedding hair off your coat. Fluff the couch. You will need to claim a corner for yourself. Tomorrow at dawn we will chase cottontails, and your shedding hair will be left on multi-floral rose and greenbrier. We won't have to groom the hair then. I will remove the briars from your coat, which will shine. We will throw away the nail trimmers—you will keep your nails at the perfect length by chasing bunnies. There will be things for supper that I do not like. You can have them. If you beg for that food in a sappy fashion I can probably give them to you directly without the house cook (the woman with the rings on her left hand) getting angry. The woman with the rings on her left hand is my boss, but don't tell her that I know it. You can sleep in the bed at night so as to make sure that I am awake plenty early to chase rabbits before work. I may be tired, but your love of the chase will overcome that sleepiness. I won't throw away the alarm clock, because the woman with the rings may need it later on in the morning after we leave. I can't chase rabbits on Sundays due to church. There may be some other mornings when we can't go. I will give you lots of food on those mornings. Typically you will eat after the morning chase. Oh, and if the boss ever brings home cube steak, you will eat a very good supper. I am the Beagle Whisperer."

...BEAUTIFULLY ON THE LINE

I was sitting comfortably in my office when my cell phone started emitting noise. It was in my book bag and I could not reach it before it stopped ringing. Immediately the office phone erupted. This only further encouraged me to consider getting rid of the cell phone, a thought I have been dwelling upon for months. My cell phone read missed call from Lenny. I answered the office phone. No one was there. I was about to dial Lenny back when my cell phone rang again.

"Hello," I said.

"Hey, it's me," replied the voice through the speaker. Now, everybody seems to say this on the phone, as if I have memorized the voice of everyone I know.

"Who?"

"Me, your wife!"

"Oh, What's up?"

"Lenny says he called your cell phone and church office and you weren't near either, so he called the house. He wants you to call him," she said.

"O.K." I called Lenny's house, there was no answer. So I called his cell phone. No answer. My cell phone rang, "Hello," I greeted the caller.

"It's me," the voice said, "You gotta give me time to answer!"

"Who is this?" I asked.

"Me!"

"Is this Lenny?" I replied.

"Yeah, that's what I said!"

"No, you said it was me," I rebutted.

"Why would I say it was you? You wouldn't call yourself!" Lenny reasoned.

"No, you said 'It's me.'" I clarified.

"No I didn't. Anyway, I read the funniest beagle article ever. Way funnier than you. I will bring it to you. Where you at?"

"At the church," I said

"No you ain't, I called there."

"You gotta give me time to answer..."

Lenny whipped into the parking lot and bounced from his truck. He was slapping his thigh and tears were streaming down his face. He could hardly breathe when he walked into the church office. He was pointing at a magazine that I did not recognize. It was not one of the beagle magazines. It was *Today's Breeder* by Purina. Lenny was pointing at an article and laughing.

"What?" I implored. He got a pen and underlined a few sentences. Actually, he scribbled over the top of some sentences while attempting to underline, due to the convulsions of his laughter. The article was about beagles. The sentences that sent Lenny into apoplectic mirth were:

The dog needs to keep his or her feet relatively still on each track and move easily while searching for the next track. Do not confuse quickness with speed in carrying the line. Some dogs can progress the line faster than others and still maintain smoothness. However, most often, trying to progress the line too quickly will result in errors caused by the dog not keeping his or her feet still.

"Ain't that the funniest thing you ever read?" Lenny said.

"Oh, those guys are serious Lenny."

"I know! that's what makes it funny! Mistakes from not keeping the feet still! HAHA. How do you chase a rabbit without moving the feet?" He slapped his thigh again and chuckled his way into his truck and drove off. I know how Lenny feels. It is a little funny, to anyone who has hunted or read the AKC rulebook definitions for the desired quality of pursuing ability, or the description for the fault of pottering. Granted, there have been attempts to modify the rulebook to allow for a really slow hound, but the rulebook still stands as a testament to hunting, despite modifications. I can remember when the rulebook stated that a hound should pursue a rabbit with the intent to overtake and kill. That has been removed. No one could watch a dog chasing with still feet and feel that they were pursuing with intent of any sort. Still feetis the nature of brace beagling though, which is what the article Lenny had read was talking about. Brace beagling is the reason why AKC is a bad word in some circles. I do own AKC beagles, from gundog stock. When I was a kid, however, most AKC registered beagles that I saw were bow legged, ponderous, and so slow that they were nicknamed walkie-talkies because they walked one step, barked a dozen times (talked) and then walked another step to repeat the process.

The morning after Lenny's visit I was running dogs and he showed up to join me for the last rabbit chase before I leashed my dogs. "HA, that was a funny article, huh?" Lenny asked

"Yeah," I said, "But those guys are serious. They think they have rulebook hounds."

"Sure, so do the guys with dogs that can't circle a rabbit solo and only bark every 100 yards as they ricochet through the woods!" Lenny said.

"You know how a brace guy described a good run to me?" I said.

"How?" Lenny laughed, thinking I was telling a joke.

"No, I am serious," I patted his back to indicate my honesty, "He said that the dog should go along until the scent gets too cold, and then stand still as it quits barking. Sorta fade off like the end of a song."

"Get outta here!" Lenny slugged me in the arm as if I told him a punch line.

"No," I insisted, "I am telling the truth. They can bark on that line in the same spot for quite a long time. That brace hound will never come close to circling the bunny, but you'd be surprised how long they can putter, sputter and crawl and still get scent. I have seen them go 20 minutes while covering 35 yards"

Lenny knew I was serious, "You're telling the truth."

"I grew up in a brace club. I had the only hunting dog on the grounds. When a brace hound barks until it runs out of scent and the line gets cold they call it "Dying beautifully on the line.""

"Shut-up!" he starting crying with laughter.

"Nope, that was a good run for the guys in my home club as a kid. That was a term they used," I said, "And the dogs can't find a rabbit. They march through the brush in skirmish lines, smashing vegetation with sawed off golf clubs to jump a rabbit for the dogs. I can't believe they are reading the same rulebook that all the gundog formats are using!"

"I know," Lenny said, "You'd think AKC could make a video that could be used at seminars where judges get licensed. They could show pottering, show babbling, show swinging. As it is now, you would think that the standards change from brace to SPO to LP, but they don't. It doesn't matter how many dogs are on the rabbit, a fault is a fault and a desired quality is a desired quality. I can see some leeway for interpretation, but..."

"And those guys get mad at us gundoggers," I said.

"Ah!" Lenny grumped, "What's the worst thing a brace beagle ever did to you?"

"I dunno." I said. "I guess one got mad at me because my dog knocked one of his dogs over."

"Really? How?" he asked.

I started to chuckle as I told him the story. I was just a kid and had my first beagle. I had never been to a field trial, and gundog trials were not to be found in PA where I grew up in the 1980's (or "way back in the nineteen hundreds") as my step-son calls it. Pennsylvania has many beagle clubs, and although the PBGA dominates now, it did not exist then—it was all brace trials. My dogs were pretty good, I thought, and dad said I could enter them in a trial if I wanted to give it a try."

"Are our dogs any good?" I begged dad.

"Well," he said, "They could stand to be a little faster. It takes good endurance too. I placed in a few trials in the 1950's but I haven't had a dog since then, until you got me back into beagles. I never had a field champion or anything.

"What's a trial like?" I asked.

"Well, they put the dogs down two at a time and the judges follow them on a horse so they don't get tired from all the running. Sometimes you see a really fast judge who

24

can run all day and he won't have a horse. All the dogs get to chase a rabbit, two beagles at a time. Then they will bring back the best ones. Then they will all run again, and they will bring back the best of those until they give out a ribbon to the best 5."

I was intrigued at the possibility. I was too young to drive a vehicle. Our home club was running a trial, and Dad happened to be off work for just one day of the two day trial. We decided to enter Princess in the 15" bitch class and Duke in the 13" dogs. I would have to find a ride to enter Duke, as Dad was not free from work that day. Even so, we were especially optimistic about Princess, as she was much quicker out of the check than Duke. And she was by far the best dog of the two at locating a rabbit.

"Must be young judges," Dad said as we pulled into the parking lot, "No horse trailers in the parking lot."

"Is that good?" I asked.

"They might see things better if they can keep up," he nodded his head in the affirmative, "But they may not have as much experience," he shook his head side to side.

We walked into the clubhouse and ordered breakfast.

"Judges must be outside," I whispered to my father, "I don't see any young people in here that could keep up on foot. No one looks fast enough to follow the dogs." I ate breakfast and dad had coffee. It was almost 8:00 a.m., the time that entries were to close. "It won't take long to whittle them down to 5 today," I said, "There is only about 10 here. Fifty-fifty chance!"

They closed the entries and introduced the judges. They definitely were not young. They were very nice to me, and told me how nice it was to see a kid at a beagle trial. Princess was in the first brace. I was excited about her running first, because the morning dew would quicken her step and help her drive the line. The air was a little cool, and sometimes she could run with her head raised up a little in such ideal scenting conditions.

I kept Princess on a leash as they instructed. She was choking herself trying to get in the brush. She had no idea why all those people were in the thickets without her! The gallery produced a rabbit and I walked over with Princess.

"Stay back," Dad said, "Don't get in front of the judges. They will have a guy called the marshal tell ya when they have seen enough."

My brace mate had bowed legs under a basset-like body. I wondered how it could run. We got to the marked line and my competitor put his dog on the line. Then Princess went behind her. The bitch I ran against took two steps, stopped, and starting barking into the ground. Blades of grass on the mowed feed strip blew backwards like those palm trees *The Weather Channel* always shows whenever a hurricane comes ashore. And then it happened--Princess went under the other dog and flipped her over. She then locked onto the scent and thundered over the hill. The other dog was on her side and rocked back and forth to get back to her feet. She resumed barking in the same spot. The judges pointed at her. No doubt, they thought the same thing I did about the other dog--She looked pretty bad on a hot line in great morning dew. I beamed with pride, thinking I had the best dog in this brace.

They ignored Princess, never followed her, and stared at her brace mate. "What tremendous tenacity in the face of adversity," the one judge said to the other."

"Yeah, you can hardly tell she was wheel-barrowed like that," said the other judge.

Princess circled the rabbit back to us. The judges hadn't seen her though. When the rabbit passed in front of the gallery, and then past my brace mate they yelled, "Marshal next brace!" My dad stood with his jaw wide open. He looked at the other dog, looked at the judges, and then looked at me.

"What happened?" I asked him.

"I have no bleepity bleeping idea," he said quietly, almost to no one. Dad used a lot of words that I am not permitted to type in a family magazine. Many of them were anatomical references and terms used to question the legitimacy of a child born out of wedlock. I took Princess back to the truck and gave her some water. She ignored the water, and wanted to chase more rabbits. The next brace started running on the marked line of the rabbit that lapped my brace mate and Princess was close enough to hear it. She whimpered and barked with excitement.

"Holy Cow!" The guy I ran dogs with yelled, "Not only did she wheel-barrow my dog but now it is barking at another brace!"

"Oh," I said, "She does that. She wants to go run with those other dogs. I will try to keep her quiet."

"Damn wind-splitter!" he hurled an insult at my dog.

"Bleep," dad insulted the guy with an anatomical reference.

As you can imagine, the trial had hounds very different from the beagles my father ran in the 1950's. His hounds then were descended from Gray's Linesman, a brace hound in his day who could really run. Princess did not place for me that day in the 80's, as you can also surmise. Duke, although more conservative than Princess, was never entered.

"He ain't as quick as Princess," I said to my father.

"He is still to bleepity bleeping quick, unless he would have an accident and break his back legs." Dad said. That is how I ended the story to Lenny.

"That's it?" He asked, "That is the worst thing a brace beagler ever did to you?"

"Well, one time I tried to join a brace club, after the gundog movement started and I moved away from home."

"And?" Lenny raised an eyebrow.

"I volunteered to mow paths, cut brush, shag rabbits and all the rest if they let me run dogs and start puppies at the running grounds," I said, "Just as I did for my home brace club as a kid. They let me run my hunting dogs on the club grounds. In exchange for working the trials"

"You get into the club?" Lenny snickered.

"They made me go to 5 or 6 meetings. Then they voted on my membership while I stood in the rain."

"How did they vote?" Lenny said.

"Well. They wouldn't tell me. They said they had to mail the result of the vote."

"They didn't even tell you to your face?"

"Nope," I said, "I got the rejection letter a week later."

"So are you mad?"

"Nah," I said. "And I am truly not angry. I am secretary and field trial secretary of that club now. It is a gundog club in the Pennsylvania Beagle Gundog Association. There are very few brace beaglers in the area now. When I look at the published trial results from a traditional brace trial, I can't imagine a dog living long enough to finish for its championship in brace trials. With a class of ten or eleven entries it must take a dozen wins to finish a hound. I figure, unless something really drastic happens, brace beagling will die beautifully on the line. Of course it may be hard to tell the difference between death and keeping the feet still. It will be nice not to have to explain to people that AKC beagles are good hunting dogs."

Just then Lenny's cell phone rang. Before he could answer it, the ringing stopped. I got my phone out and was ready this time. "Hello?" I answered. "Yep, he is right here," I handed the phone to his wife "It's your wife." I might get rid of that phone yet. I have no desire to be Lenny's answering service.

DULCIMERS AND THE DOG DAYS OF SUMMER

September marks the beginning of the return to normalcy in my house. There are certainly advantages to having hunting house hounds—I think the beagles handle better, and they can double as wonderful pets. But it is this pet component of their personality that causes summer chaos. You see, the damn dogs are cute. They are also stubborn, and have managed to claim the furniture, the yard, and most of my hunting socks. The same persistence that allows them to run a rabbit until it goes in a hole or is killed has also enabled the dogs to train me to arise before dawn and take them to the field for a morning session of cottontail therapy. They begin their alarm clock efforts over an hour before dawn with a series of pathetic whimpers, indicating that they are awake and bored without any humans walking around. These whimpers are the equivalent of an opera singer going through voice exercises. The low whispery whimpers then give way to sporadic, but loud, yips. Sometimes I will try to sleep through the yips, and the result is a chorus of howls. At this point I get out of bed because my wife only howls once or twice before she slaps me on the arm with a backhand (sometimes the backhand lands on my face) while clutching her pillow to her ears. The dogs go out into the fenced yard for their morning bathroom break, and then wait beside the door that leads to the truck, heads on their paws, while I drink coffee. When I reach for my boots tail wags thump out a cacophony of noise against the linoleum floor that rivals the intensity of the traveling percussion band named Stomp. Rabbit running then ensues.

July and August are horrible disruptions of this morning routine, a routine that happens almost every day before I go to work. The heat and high humidity preclude forays afield most summer mornings. Even though the dogs are willing to run in such conditions it is dangerous for them, and not pleasurable for me. Bug bites, sunburns, and general crankiness plague me when running in the dog days of summer. It is at this point, each year that I turn the happy house beagles into criminals; or that is their feeling about the matter, anyway. They begin to see the house and yard as a prison that prevents access to rabbits. They take out their aggression on chipmunks dumb enough to stroll into the yard. A few beagles can handle a chipper chipmunk faster than a cat could possibly do the same. One beagle blocks access to the tree and the others set upon the hapless rodent like a pride of lions on a gazelle. Speaking of stray cats, they are normally treated with fairly benign indifference by the pack, but after several weeks without any cottontail therapy the dogs begin to see the felines in the same way I see deer—something to hunt when I can't pursue rabbits. They will tree the neighbor's house cat and then wait under the tree for the quarry to descend on an escape attempt. All of these behaviors are categorized as tolerated inmate behavior.

After the summer incarceration drags on more than a month, their behavior becomes problematic. They will attempt to tunnel under the fence, or maybe even go over it. They may wait beside the door and hope that someone entering the home does not notice their slipping outside as the person comes in. Remember what I said about how well the house beagle handles afield? It is not true on a jailbreak. A hunting house beagle is pleased to go afield and chase rabbits, and will listen well on the hunt, knowing that the purpose of the trip is the chasing of bunnies. A beagle-inmate on the lam will not listen to even the most basic commands. He is free and wants to jump game. Such a beast will forget all morals and behave like someone who has gone to some den of sin--a place like Las Vegas, or New Jersey. If more than one inmate escapes the confinement of the yard, they will only encourage one another to commit increasingly sinful acts, and will come home with their white bellies covered in dried mud and their breath smelling like they found something rotten to snack upon. On such escapes there are the obvious dangers of roads and cars.

There is the additional concern that such beagles are mostly non-discriminating as it regards the species of game that they chase. Ferrell cats, squirrels that have strayed from a tree line, or even a deer are potential running mates. If the jailbreak is nocturnal, opossums, porcupines, and skunks are potential targets for a frustrated rabbit dog. A skunk sprayed dog immediately goes into the solitary confinement quarters (the garage) until multiple outdoor baths with various homemade and purchased remedies takes place over several days. When said skunk runner returns to the actual house he always has a tale for the other incarcerated beagles, "I was free man, I had brush against my belly and scent in my muzzle. It was worth the four days in the hole. These screws can't keep me inside, I will get out again." One of the disadvantages of house beagles is that they watch television and learn prison lingo. If, on some warm evening I would opt to go hunt groundhogs in order to help a local farmer, I might hear one say something like "Go hunting without me? I will shank you!" More prison lingo.

At this point most of my fence bottom is encased in cement. They must have a system wherein two beagles engage in cute behaviors and cuddling with a human while a third beast begins tunneling under the freedom denying fence or "The wall" as the dogs call it. I will discover the excavation project and fill it with ready mix cement. The local hardware store employees probably think I am a bricklayer, given the volume of cement that I purchase. When it goes on sale I buy a bag and store it in the solitary confinement quarters. The resulting moats of concrete are good for keeping the hounds' nails trimmed, as they try digging through cement with futile optimism. I rarely need to trim a dogs nails—regular chases and the prison yard cement keep the toes looking neat and clean.

Sometimes, I will sit in the yard with the beagles and allow them to expend their boundless energy running around the charcoal grill while I cook supper. The grill is obviously too hot for them to touch with their noses, but they will circle it like sharks, sniffing the smoke as it spews into the air and drifts throughout the yard. At times, this can distract them from planning future escapes for a couple hours as I prepare supper. My wife thinks that cooking ribs is very difficult. This is mostly because she lacks the patience required to ignore the meat for an hour as it slow cooks in the airless environment of a covered grill without being touched or flipped. She feels a need to open the lid, and the rush of air causes the coals to flare high and burn the meat. She just puts too much effort into the act of outdoor cooking. The same thing also happens with houseplants, which often meet an early demise from being loved with too much water. Our home is where ferns go to die.

When cooking ribs, I simply go out into the yard and strum a few tunes on the mountain dulcimer while sitting under the shade tree. Ninety percent of cooking ribs is simply knowing enough songs on the dulcimer to pick tunes for an hour while they cook. The other ten percent is having a shade tree to utilize while keeping one eye on the grill in the event that a particularly clever beagle devises a way to get the food away from the heat; or an especially stubborn dog shows signs of a willingness to burn itself while toppling the grill over to abscond with the pork treat. In fact, the dog days of summer often find me sitting under the tree and playing tunes in the early morning as well, when it is as cool as it will be all day. I often play the blues for the beagles as they pace the perimeter of the "rock." That is another bit of prison lingo the pack has learned from television. Playing the dulcimer in the morning is a poor substitute for conditioning hounds, but it allows me to learn a few new songs every summer. My beagle training hat is soaked with the DEET insecticide, and I wear it as the dogs and I sit in the lawn and dream of cooler days to come.

The dogs prefer to hear the mountain dulcimer in the evenings, after a successful morning afield and the completion of the work day. As September rounds the corner, it is time for the beagles to begin their stay in partial incarceration, aka the beagle club. I will take them to the running grounds, where there is a rabbit rich environment and few worries of deer. It takes a couple chases to get the pack back into some semblance of order. They need to work off the energy and settle into their rhythm of the chase. But September is here, and that means that the dews have returned to the morning ground, and the air has a little biting chill in the evening. It makes a beagle, and its owner, think of hunting. September also produces daydreaming. I think of road trips to states that allow hunting earlier than my beloved Keystone State, which does not commence rabbit hunting until the end of October.

It is only during rabbit season that the mountain dulcimer can express the fullness of joy. Properly speaking, a dulcimer is a sort of evening dessert for my ears. A good evening has the fireplace burning as I clean a favorite double barrel shotgun. If it is a really good day I will find only one dirty barrel, indicating that I never needed the second shot to kill a rabbit. I clean the second barrel anyway, of course, as the scent of Hoppes wafts amongst the smell of the fireplace. Tired beagles sprawl across the hardwood floor, staring into the fire while the flames reflect in their eyes, as if they remember some primal era when they were still wolves and we hunters still lived in caves and other structures as we followed the game. When the gun is cleaned and a cup of tea is consumed, I will break out the dulcimer and softly fingerpick a few tunes while the hounds gradually relax their steady gaze, which is fixed upon the undulating fire. Slowly the beagles close their eyes and the fire is no longer visible in reflection through their brown eyelids. They produce a gentle snore that provides a soft backbeat to the dulcimer. Then tiny paws begin to flail as they remember the day's hunt in their dreams and the scent of rabbits fills their souls anew. When the dream gets to a particularly exciting part of the hunt, they will sometimes bark themselves awake in the full cry of pursuit and run about the house looking for the rabbit. Yes, those great evenings will be here soon. For now, however, we are just entering the halfway house of the beagle club, and I must put the dulcimer, and this computer, away; as I think I see an attempted jailbreak happening on the eastern wall. I better fire up the grill. Ribs will be ready in an hour, bring something cold and meet me under the tree if you want.

ALREADY ON THE MOUNTAIN

The church I serve has a lot of Eagle Scouts. What I mean by that is there seem to be several new ones minted each year, at which time there is great fanfare, ceremony, and feasting. Usually a local dignitary—or sometimes a dignitary-wannabee—will say a few special words. My job at such functions is fairly simple, usually consisting of an opening prayer at the ceremony, a benediction after the bestowal of accolades and honors, and a blessing over the food. There are an abundance of such social gatherings where the main role of the clergyman is to prayer over the food. I am not sure why my prayers are deemed more appropriate than others, but they are. I suppose if no pastor was present then no one would eat. Or maybe there would be a mad dash for the food line. The fact remains that there are many groups that never seem to need clergy assistance for anything, other than a prayer over the food. The Scouts, however, are active in the church and they use our building. Some kids even have badges that are earned by studying their faith. I try to make as many of their events as they might need me to attend.

At any rate, I can see why our kids stick with scouting long enough to achieve the lofty title of Eagle Scout, as their troop is always doing fun things. They take rafting trips lasting several days in duration down the Susquehanna River, go winter camping and compete against other troops in snow sports, learn rappelling and rock climbing, and embark on many other high adventures. I may have become an Eagle Scout, if such things were scheduled activities when I was a kid. I only served a one year hitch in the scouts, and it was as a Cub. My memory is vague, but I believe I would have been in second or third grade, whatever the youngest age for scouting was at the time. I was looking forward to my enlistment in the scouts, as I had seen a video at school that detailed rugged outdoor activities. Rugged outdoor activities always appealed to me, probably because I was scrawny and wore thick glasses. Even so, I was an avid outdoorsman (or outdoors-boy) who loved to fish and tag along with whatever relatives would take me afield during hunting season.

I showed up at the first Cub Scout meeting with my uniform unkempt and a mustard stain on my blue jeans. My perpetual appearance as a child was skinny with an un-tucked shirt tail and a mustard stain on my pants. I am happy to report that after all these years my appearance has changed since then—I am no longer skinny. Anyway, it was no matter that I was disheveled in appearance since I already knew the names of over a dozen trees from walks in the woods with my father. And from stacking firewood. Dad would split the firewood and it was my job to gather the scattered halves and quarters and then neatly arrange them as high as I could reach. Later, my dad would raise the walls of cordwood that ringed the perimeter of our yard higher than I could reach with additional loads of spit firewood, providing a "walled compound" look to our property. The compound walls were then burned as the winter drug on into spring. No doubt you have seen houses with the windows wide open in autumn and spring. That is what happens when you burn firewood and the mornings are frigid and the afternoons are hot.

"What kinda tree is that?" I would ask as the log splintered under the axe.

"Ash," Dad would answer. It turned out that most of the trees were ash, because they split so easy, as I would learn in a few years when dad handed over the wood-splitting chore to me. Still, there were a few other types of wood mixed in, usually twisted and knotted.

"Look at that one there, what is that?" I would follow up with another question.

"Maple," came the response. And so it would go. I considered myself quite the scholar of trees. I was hoping that the first scout meeting was going to focus on trees.

"What's your name?" the Den Mother asked me at my first meeting

"Bob," I answered, "And I am ready to identify trees tonight, so long as they are the kind that ya burn in the woodstove. I am still not good at all the evergreens."

"I thought we would just do a craft tonight," the Den Mother said, a cigarette bouncing in her lips.

I was crestfallen. Scouts met on a Wednesday, the same day that I had art class at school. I did not like art. I wasn't good at it. Wednesday became art day, first at school and then at scouts. Have you ever seen those religious crosses that people make by gluing a million kitchen matches together into an elaborate cross? The kind where the match was lit just long enough to burn away the flammable tip before being blown out? My Cub Scout den probably made most of those cross decorations found east of the Mississippi. I thought that I had enlisted in the scouts, but it was really a sweat shop for crafts, many of which had a religious bent. There were match crosses for weeks. We also made plastic mesh refrigerator magnets with the word JESUS in capital block letters in one color of yarn with the background in another color. Normally Black letters and a gold background—it was Pittsburgh Steelers country, after all. There is a not-so-subtle fusion of football and religion in Western Pennsylvania that I am sure exists in other locales as well. We also made Bible covers. Then there were secular crafts as well.

Even on the rare instances that we did not make crafts, we still stayed inside and only studied outdoor activities from a book. I had saved money to buy a cheap compass, and it was of no use—we never left the woman's house! I had a sleeping bag. We had one camping trip—in the Den Mother's living room! I wanted to quit. One day I was stacking firewood for Dad, and thought I would breach the subject of quitting the scouts. I thought it best to start with small talk, "Hey Dad, what kinda tree is that?" I asked as a piece of wood was splintered in half.

"How many damn times do I have to tell you? It is ash!" Such was parenting in the '70s.

"So," I said, "I'm gonna quit scouts if that's OK?"

He was just raising the axe and had reached the Zenith of his arc. He paused, holding the axe high, and turned his head to look at me as I stood off to the side. "What?" he glared.

"I hate it. All we do is make crafts for the Den Mother's relatives. By the way, what is a quota? She says that word a lot."

He slowly lowered the ax. What else do you do besides crafts?"

"Nothing," I said, "Some of the mothers stick around and eat desserts, smoke cigarettes, and talk while we work on the crafts, but it is basically a second art class for me."

"Yeah you can quit," he said, and my hart leaped, "At the end of the year," he clarified, and my heart sank. I toughed out the year. I painted a bunch of ceramic pumpkins at Halloween, made little turkey replicas for Thanksgiving, assembled about 20 Christmas ornaments, and painted about a dozen hollowed eggs as Easter decorations. Sally Struthers should have found us and lent her weight to our cause. We finally did make it outside at the end of the year—into the Den Mother's back yard for a hotdogs and roasted marshmallows. At the end of the year I ran like an AWOL sailor on shore leave and never went back.

Several years later I heard that the guys who stuck through the hard years actually got to go camping and do some other fun things. By then I was into beagles. But I also was quite keen on the book (and the movie) called *My Side of the Mountain*. Many probably are familiar with the tale, but if not it is about a boy who runs off to do algae experiments in the woods, alone, for a prolonged time period; and lives in a hollow tree. I was eager to find a hollow tree to live inside. The author of the book, Jean Craighead George, didn't indicate that such a tree would be quite hard to find, and even harder to hollow out as the book's main character had done. I decided to make a tree fort instead, which was the standard shelter for all kids back then.

Basically, we found somebody's old tree stand, and kept expanding the structure until there were enough boards nailed to the tree to ensure that it would never be a prime lumber tree. My tree fort was waterproof with the addition of a piece of corrugated fiberglass that I managed to lay my hands upon and add to the roof. Now all I had to do was run away and live there. The kid in the book had a falcon that hunted for him, I had a couple beagles. Running away in rural Pennsylvania was different back then. We lived right next to the woods and played in them all day. No one asked where we might be. People just presumed that, in the summer, we would come home when we got hungry. This was in the age when adults filled all public spaces with cigarette smoke (Den Mothers chained smoked in your face) and no one wore seat belts. In school teachers would walk out of the teacher's lounge and massive plumes of cigarette smoke would billow out into the hallway. Paddling was a daily occurrence in the hallways. We played tag football in the street as there wasn't much traffic in a small town residential neighborhood until the factory changed shifts.

Teachers could not catch the kids who smoked in high school because everybody smelled like smoke all the time—from walking in the barbershop or the garage or almost anywhere. When people drank too much beer the cops pulled them over and drove them home, so help me it seems unreal to the youngsters, but this is how it was then. So, when I made my runaway attempt, no one noticed until after suppertime--long after suppertime because my family presumed that I had eaten at some friend's house.

I had run away to live at the tree fort in the morning. No one noticed until late at night. I had packed survival rations: Two peanut butter and Jelly sandwiches, a few cans of *Chef-Boyardee* ravioli, and some dog food for the beagles. I figured I had enough provisions to last until the beagles could get some rabbits. The beagles were right on the job chasing a bunny pretty steadily around the tree fort. I was planning on building a slingshot to try and shoot a rabbit from the actual tree fort. By nightfall I had made quick work of all the provisions, and I was full, but out of food. I fed the dogs which had exhausted themselves on the rabbit. They did not catch the bugger, and I was starting to wonder if a falcon (like the kid in the book had) might not have been the better way to go. I tied the dogs to some saplings at the base of the tree fort to keep them close by for the night. As night fell, the woods came alive.

A chipmunk, on dry leaves, sounds a lot like a bear. A possum, running on dry leaves, sounds like several bears. A deer, walking through the area and then sprinting after the dogs bark, sounds like—you guessed it, a bear. I decided that I needed a fire for the night, so that I would not be scared any longer. I was good at building fires with matches. I had lit and blown out boxes of kitchen matches for the purpose of constructing pious crosses, remember? My rock ring was plenty safe to prevent a forest fire. I did not want to see Smokey the Bear, because after all, he was a bear. There is a tradition in rural Pennsylvania, and no doubt other places, where the night before the biggest football game against the arch-rival school is celebrated with a bonfire. The whole town gathers around this pyrotechnic spectacle. Old jocks tell stories of games from their youth against the same school, and people enjoy the spirit of competition. You can see for a long ways under the light of a football bonfire. Such a fire was a mere kindling flame compared to my bear-fire. It was only after this pyre was roaring that I could see that there were no bears, but only small rodents and the stray deer or two. About 11 p.m., I heard some crunching coming up behind me. I turned to look without fear, confident that no bear would approach. I saw the source of the noise and panic gripped me.

"Well, you sure did find a lot of dead ash trees," Dad said, "What are you doing?"

"I ran away. How long you been looking for me?" I asked, still afraid that I was in trouble

"'Bout a half hour," he said, "I saw the glow. What'd ya run away from?" He asked.

"Oh nothing, I just wanted to study nature and get my own food. Like the kid in *My Side of the Mountain*."

"In where?" He asked.

"It's a book," I said, "where this kid gets sick of living in the city and runs away to the woods."

"I see, well you don't live in a city, do ya?"

"I guess not," I conceded, "but I gotta get to the woods."

"Hell, boy," he said, "The woods are everywhere! You are already on the mountain."

"I guess so!" I rejoiced, realizing that nature was always close at hand.

"I will take these dogs back and tell your mother that I found you. I will come back then, cuz we are gonna hafta stay till this fire burns out. You want some supper?" He asked, looking at the empty cans of ravioli.

"Maybe a snack if you want to share one," I said.

"I will be back," and off he went to soothe and comfort my mother. Dad returned a bit later with some cheese, crackers, root beer, and real beer. We talked all night until the fire was burned down low enough to walk home. He encouraged me to keep reading books, and even to write a bit if I wanted.

A couple years ago I went for a walk to check on a friend of mine who was one of the chaperones for the local scout troop on a camping trip. I went there in the morning just to see how everyone had fared through the night. The campfire was burning at a nice level for cooking breakfast.

"You built a good fire this morning," I said to one of the kids as I arrived.

"Ha!" he said, "that fire is left over from last night!"

"Ohhh," I scratched my chin, "Did you see a bear?"

"Yeah!" the kid shrieked, "How did you know?"

"Lucky guess."

A BEAGLER'S SNOW DAY

Happy New Year! I love winter, and that is why I look forward to January. We are now into the time of year when rabbit hunters can have a bit more success. The snow has knocked down the goldenrod and other vegetations, and the invisible rabbits will now stand out on the white ground cover as they dart between one hiding spot and the next. Of course this is also the time of year when we hunt snowshoe rabbits in Pennsylvania, although it is a short season. The hare are white regardless of the weather, and snow cover makes the hunt enjoyable. There are few things as exhilarating as shooting hare on the snow, and few things as unsatisfying as shooting a pure white hare which is standing stark still, in the belief that it is invisible, as it crouches on hemlock needles. The animal is as obvious as any other white object on a green and brown surface.

It is also a wonderful time to be in the woods because the rifle season for deer is over. Don't get me wrong, I deer hunt too, but I get annoyed at the crowds of people in the woods for those two weeks. January marks the beginning of most of our bigger snow accumulations. By far the best part of winter is snow days. Snow days are more common now than they once were. When I was a child there had to be a blizzard before the schools would cancel classes. I still remember people driving rear wheel drive cars uphill in reverse with the driver door open to enable clear visibility as the person driving the car would look out the door and steer one-handed to make adjustments to the slipping and sliding of the automobile. The vehicle seemed to get better traction in reverse, and if you were unable to get to the top and had to go down the hill the operator could slam the door shut and navigate the treacherous descent with both hands while looking out the front windshield. Backward descents were quite miserable, hence the reverse climbs. Alas, the abundance of four wheel drive vehicles has taken the fun out of winter travel.

Snow days are now common enough that even the hardier schools in the lake effect snow belt will frequently delay or cancel. I, for my part, have taken a stand of solidarity with the school teachers. When they are off work due to weather I also stay home. Quite a supporter of education, aren't I? That's the level of my commitment. No need to thank me, I am happy to do it. This brings us to the issue of preparing for the big snow. If at all possible, it is best to buy provisions for a beagler's snow day well in advance. Going to the grocery store the night before the snow is a fiasco, as everyone stocks up on bread, milk, and toilet paper. People fill their carts with those three items! I say if bread and milk affect one's gastrointestinal system in such an adverse fashion that 20 rolls of toilet paper are necessary, then perhaps a better survival food should be found.

If, however, you are stuck in the supermarket the night before the big blast, then there are a few things that you should remember. First, don't buy milk or bread. This is a potential day off. Make it enjoyable. My snow day meal of choice is rabbit stew. So I buy the essential ingredients for the stew: bacon, onions, mushrooms, chicken broth, tomato paste, carrots, potatoes and spinach. I get some fancy potato just for the occasion—I like those yellow ones. Next, I go to the dairy aisle and get some really expensive cheese and some half and half. I once started a frenzy by selecting half and half at the market.

"What are you getting?!" a woman shrieked as she saw me load the carton into the cart, "I need some of that too!" And with that the entire aisle flocked to the half and half and bought it. Exercise caution when selecting your ingredients. I also like to get some brand name cola, good ice cream, and cornbread mix. It is important to whistle and show joy as you fill your cart. Many in the store are panicked, so I walk slowly down the aisles (dare I say, I saunter) and I smile and wave. This pleasant attitude helps me protect myself from the carts that are slamming into each other. Whatever you do, don't go over the express lane limit of items in your cart. People are stocking up on supplies and the express lane is the only way out of that place! I usually come in right at the express lane limit. This yields a short line and a leisurely drive home to prepare for the big day off.

I debone 10-12 rabbits and place the meat in the refrigerator. When I awake in the morning I am always so happy to see the snow piling up against the storm door. I throw the meat into the crock pot with the tomato paste, potatoes, carrots, and spinach. In a frying pan I cook 5 pieces of bacon until it is crisp and break those into the stew. Feel free to cook extra strips to eat for breakfast. A big onion and the mushrooms then get diced, cooked in the bacon fat, and added to the pot. You can then cover the whole batch in chicken broth and add whatever seasonings get you going! I use lots of black pepper, garlic, basil, and a splash of Old Bay.

Now that the food is safely cooking in the slow cooker, have a cup of coffee with the half and half. Sometimes I get raw milk from a farm and use that instead. I scoop the fatty cream off the top of the container that has sat in the fridge over night. While drinking coffee, I begin to get the beagles excited. I might grab a leash, pick up my boots, or grab a shotgun. Once a belly full of hot coffee is warming me against the cold, I go ahead and load up some pooches for a short hunt. The roads are free and clear as people panic and stay home. The woods are empty of most people, and great chases can be had in a snow storm that isn't too windy. If the snow is falling sideways the hunt is often bad. Great chases, however, can be had on a day that finds great big snowflakes falling perpendicular to the earth under calm winds.

After a few bunnies are harvested, I load the dogs up and call home from my cell phone. I like to have Renee throw my big comfy pajama bottoms, thick socks, and a soft flannel shirt into the clothes dryer, even though they are already clean and dry. Next I clean and soak the rabbits before bringing the dogs into the house and heading straight for the basement. I strip to the bone and take the warm clothes out of the dryer. When you are wet and cold from waiting for the rabbits to circle in a snow storm those clothes feel wonderful. And they have a

function too, as this is when the hot stew is eaten! Comfy
pajama bottoms allow for expansion of the midsection
under the feast. Renee's cornbread finishes off the
delicacy. Washed down with Pepsi, it is a perfect meal on a
day off.

At this point it is essential to resist the temptation to
shovel the sidewalk. Wait until the snow blast is actually
over. Remember, there is still some cheese to slice and
enjoy as a snack in a little while, after the rabbit is
digested. Following the cheese, it is a great time to sit by
the fireplace and clean the shotgun while sipping a second
Pepsi. We no longer have a fireplace, but we do have a
pellet stove. In fact, we have the wood pellet stove because
fireplace had a small fire. What do I mean by small?

Well, I called 911 one fine morning a dew winters ago
and expressed concern that there were puffs of smoke
coming through the cracks of the paneling on the wall that
held the fireplace. Four fire trucks showed up, and they
had to re-route traffic to the school. It was embarrassing,
but they were doing their job. They brought in a thermal
detecting doohickey that found the heat behind the
fireplace, which had been used briefly the night before.
They quickly smashed the mantle and ripped apart the
wall and put the fire out with 8 gallons of water. We had
minimal fire or water damage, and the fire department was
great. Honest, they told me it was 8 gallons of water! The
insurance company replaced the fireplace with a wood
pellet stove because the old chimney was not up to modern
code, and they refinished all the hardwood floors in the
downstairs. The living room is quite pleasant. It is a great
place to sit with the beagles and clean the gun as the dogs
slumber beside the "fireplace" and run the chases anew in
their dreams.

The day I just described gets lived several times each
winter. In fact, it was after just such a day that I decided
to write to a few publishers. I explained in my letters that I
had written all of these beagle articles (many of which were
in another magazine) and that I was trying to get a book
published. I think I wrote to four or five publishers.
Sunbury Press, located in my home state, was very excited
at the possibility that a collection of my stories could be

made into a book. I was elated! I probably never would have tried to get published if I could have gone to work that day. I am thrilled to say that a second book should be available by the time you read this article. The first book did well enough to justify a sequel. I will save this story for a third book, if I get to have it published. If you look at the cover of *Beagle Tales 2*, you will see the wood pellet stove that I just mentioned. It is a reminder to me that snow days are magic. I want to thank everyone who has written me a kind word or ordered a book. It is truly an honor to write for *The American Beagler* each month. Janie asked me to write for the magazine after Sunbury Press sent her a copy of the first book. I hope you have a great New Year, and cherish those snow days! Go ahead and try my beagler's snow day. After the gun is cleaned and you fall asleep in front of the stove with the dogs you will wake up and be a little warm. That's when you get the ice cream that I mentioned in the earlier grocery list. Enjoy the day, work comes tomorrow.

SPRING WATER

When I was a child, spring water came from springs.
This is a remarkable revelation to youngsters nowadays,
who think that spring water comes from plastic bottles. If
you would have told me that people would pay money for
spring water at convenience stores when I was a kid I
would have never believed such a lie. I try to avoid buying
water, but I have to admit there have been a few occasions
when I left the house without a jug of water to cool down
the pooches after a few hours of pounding the rabbit
tracks. A typical solution to this rare event is to leash the
hounds and lead them to a creek or mud puddle, but there
have been dry days where I had to buy bottled water. I
have no idea why beagles love the taste of mud puddles,
but it seems to be as true as the fact that they love to eat
miscellaneous rotting animal matter if chance should
provide such a morsel.

Anyway, fetching spring water was a common chore
during my youth, and we would load up the truck with
empty plastic juice/milk containers and drive off to a
spring. Many people grew up consuming well water, and
did not like the taste of chlorinated "city water" even if the
city was more like a small town or a scattered collection of
tiny villages. So, a common enough summer venture was
to go fill the jugs with ice cold spring water and then stop
for soft serve ice cream on the way home.

Of course these sorties for high quality H2O became
drudgery as one entered the realm of teenage years. Just
when a guy had plans to hunt, play baseball, or go talk to
some girls (the newly found joy of joys that everyone denied
wanting to do), there would be an order to load plastic jugs
into the truck. Now, I should clarify that, by and large,
spring water tasted like spring water, which is to say that
you could not taste the massive amounts of chlorination
that sometimes saturated the municipal water, especially

when it rained. One spring tasted mostly identical to another. They had no taste, really. Most adults, however, had specific springs that were the only source of water that would be collected for them. As a kid I accompanied several different families to several different springs while visiting friends. So long as the spring did not dry up in the summer it was clearly good, clean, and cold ground water-- the sort of springs that have made Pennsylvania famous for spring-fed trout water streams, cool in the summer but ice free in the winter as the waters gurgle from the earth.

The spring that I used most frequently was at the beagle club. There was a spring house that was set up to gather water for canines and humans. As the crow flies it was not all that far from one of the municipal water supplies, a small creek that my father once fished for native brook trout before it was dammed to collect domestic water. The beagle club did not have the most powerful spring, and hence took some time to fill a jug, but its pressure stayed constant all year and no one was using it for more than watering the dogs after a summer chase or for drinking a few gulps yourself as the beagles panted in the shade with a bowl of the same water. A tin cup rested nearby for communal use. It just so happened that we often ran dogs every day in the summer, until it was too hot to do so.

When I was 15 my friend Stump, was 16. Not only was he old enough to drive, he had a license. Not only did he have a license, he also had a pickup truck. Stump's grandfather owned beagles, and I did too. We would spend summer evenings running beagles at the club, a chore for which we could get a little gas money from my father. This was a rarity, as dad mostly forced me to buy things with my own money from a paper route and other odd jobs. Running dogs was one thing that dad felt kept me out of trouble, and he would finance dog training with gas money. That being said, remember, this was an era when no one considered fuel efficiency or gasoline prices. It seemed endlessly cheap and abundant, and when you filled a lawnmower and it spilled over the top it was just collateral loss. Seeing gas spill over the fill cap now makes me think, "There goes 50 cents."

It was not uncommon for dad to give us five dollars for gas money to run dogs. Brace yourself if you are a teenager reading this article: that was over a half tank of gasoline in a pickup truck. Stump and I began to calculate how far we could go with five dollars. Soon we had discovered that we could do the following: (1) load his grandfather's dogs in his truck. (2) Load my dogs in the truck. (3) Let the dogs chase rabbits until dusk. (4) Return my dogs to my house. (5) Return his grandpa's dogs. (6) Tell his family we had to go unload my dogs, even though we already had done so, and (7) Go somewhere with the free gas money!

Usually we went somewhere to talk to girls. This always seemed to work better in neighboring towns where the girls didn't realize that we were just as awkward and unpopular as the boys in their own town. The ruse worked so long as Stump's family thought we were at my house after unloading my dogs, and my family thought we were at Stump's grandparents' house unloading his dogs. All hell broke loose when my ever suspicious mother would try to track me down. This was back in the B.C. years—Before Cell phones. Mom would call Stump's grandparents. Then she would call his parents. If that failed she would call other people who may have seen Stump's truck glide past their house. Actually, they may have heard it as rock and roll music blared from the very powerful stereo system. Music was communal then, and it was shared, most people having their best sound system in their vehicle as opposed to an iPod with tiny ear microphones that personalize music into a solitary experience. Teenagers of the 1980's drove with windows down, announcing their presence and identity by the style of music that oozed from the car over the sound of the exhaust. In the winter young drivers would put the heater on high and roll down the windows so as to share their musical choice even in frigid weather (Yes, it makes no sense, I know). Stump's truck oozed guitar solos at breakneck tempos. Mom always found us.

One solution to this dilemma was to keep the dogs with us as we pursued social engagements. If we never went home from the beagle club, no one thought we were into mischief. At first glance it might seem that we would skip running dogs altogether and merely load them into the truck before roaring off in pursuit of young love with the ladies. No, this was not an option. Have you ever tried to woo a young woman while a beagle whined with anticipation of rabbit chases in the bed of your truck? One of two things would happen. Either the smelly beast caused too much confusion and chaos to allow wooing, or the girls would see the beagles and they forgot about us as they gushed over the beagles. At first we thought we might convince the girls to run dogs in the woods with us, but they were mostly interested in rubbing the beagles belly and giving them attention, rather than entering the brush to watch the dogs chase a cute rabbit. Still, the cute beagles could be an inroad to feminine conversation and I can still remember bathing beagles to get the hound odor off of the beasts in case an attractive young gal would want to see the beast. Nothing, I feared, could make such a gal have a lower opinion of me than the dog jumping on her lap to self-disclose the odor of the cow flop that he rolled in the previous week. A giant stain of dust from the dried mud of a hunting beagle's coat would be equally disastrous as the beautiful maiden walked away with a trailing cloud of debris a la Pig-Pen from Charlie Brown. Nope, we ran the dogs hard to get them tired, so that they would sleep in the crates as we strutted like peacocks.

It was in pursuit of such ventures that Stump and I had a spring water incident. His grandmother, Agnes, was low on spring water. She gave us 20 dollars to go fill the water jugs at her favorite spring on Horner Road, which was a little ways away. We were to take her vehicle, a Chevy Blazer, fill the gas tank when we returned with the water, and pocket the remaining money for ourselves. We quickly opened the hatch on the back of the Blazer and loaded the jugs into the back. We pulled out of the driveway and headed in the direction of Horner Road. Then we turned onto a street out of the sight line of Agnes' house and traveled in the opposite direction.

"Where we goin?" I asked.

"To get spring water," Stump said, "Duh, we have jugs in the back."

"Yeah, but Horner Road isn't out this way." I clarified.

"Right."

"Sooo," I thought out loud, "Where are we going?"

"To the beagle club."

"Why?" I squinted an eye in confusion.

"Cuz it's a lot closer and we will have even more extra money left over for our own travels in my truck!" Stump beamed with delight in his own plan.

"You, my friend," I patted him on the shoulder, "Are an evil genius."

It was a hot, dry summer. We started filling the jugs at the beagle club spring house. We placed all the empty jugs near the spring. I was kneeling and filling jugs. Stump was carrying the full ones to the Blazer. It was a slow process as only one jug could be filled at a time from the small spring. Suddenly I slapped my arm, "Ouch, darnit!" Only I didn't day darn it.

"What?" Stump looked at me as if I were a wimp with a fictitious pain."

"Something bit me," I said.

"Yeah, right," he doubted.

"No, I was bit—OUCH!" I slapped my arm, and there, under my palm, was a ground hornet.

"Ground hornet," I said to Stump, who looked at me as if I was teasing. I loved to tease him about snakes, biting insects, poison ivy, and any other outdoor malady you can imagine, just to get him worried. He no longer believed me about anything. Just then my back felt as if hot coals were being dumped down my shirt and Stump's eyes looked like half-dollars as he stared at me in horror. He sprinted to the blazer, slammed the back hatch and entered the driver side door a la Dukes of Hazard through the opened window. Before I knew it he was in reverse and doing a power slide to vacate the area. I dove into the passenger side just in time to make the getaway. To this day he and I argue over whether or not he had intentions of escaping with me or alone. He claims that his plan was to drive closer to me in order to facilitate a quicker escape. Given the fact that I had to dive into the window as it was quartering away from me, I feel he was trying to leave me there as a sacrificial victim to the ground hornets. Had the beagle club parking lot been paved I may have never gotten into the Blazer. The parking lot was fine silt and gravel, so he was spinning in place as he tromped on the gas pedal, giving me a few seconds to plunge into the open window as the vehicle fish-tailed away, gaining traction as it left. We were launched like a rocket as the blazer left the parking lot and gripped the paved road.

We arrived at Agnes' house without spring water, our tails tucked between our legs. My back throbbed, and looked like a combination of measles, chickenpox, and sunburn all at once.

"Gram," I said to Agnes, who treated me as her own, "How bad is it?" I had taken my shirt off in the Blazer to ensure that no Hornets were in there. It turns out they had stung me through the thin, cotton white T-shirt.

"What happened?" She fell all over me with sympathy and love and compassion.

We told her everything in the hopes that she had some remedy to the pain and poison coursing through my body. Apparently, stinging insects are the one allergy I have never had, which is good or I might have died. We could not count the welts because there were so many spots where I had been attacked. I have heard of similar swarms killing small beagles. As we told the story of the clubhouse spring, gravel parking lot, and ground hornets she interrupted us. "Whaddya mean you were at the beagle club?"

"Oh Shoot," I thought to myself. Grandmother compassion gave way to outrage at adolescent deceit.

"Boys, go get my jugs!" She entered her house and left us standing in the yard. I was shirtless and wounded from head to waist. Somehow I felt I had it better than Stump, given the punishment I imagined resulting from our failure to get water at Horner Road.

The long distance bug sprays were relatively new then, and we grabbed both cans of wasp spray from Agnes' house. I put my shirt on and walked as normally as possible to get the can of insecticide in my dad's shed. We arrived at the beagle club parking lot, greeted by the ruts that had been left in our wake.

"You gonna go down there and get the jugs?" I asked.

"Heck no!" Stump said, only he didn't say heck.

"I'm already stung!" I argued

"Exactly," he reasoned, "What if I am allergic to them?"

"Are you?"

"Dunno."

I somehow felt he was tricking me, but having been plagued with every other allergy in the world I felt obligated to help someone else—even if the allergy was unconfirmed, and no doubt a lie created to avoid pain. The hornets were still hovering over their den. Stump parked close to the hornet lair, and, through a slightly opened window, began to lay down suppressing fire upon them from the watery jet of wasp spray. They retreated into the ground.

"Better get them jugs quick," he said. I scampered to the jugs and began tossing them into the back seat of the Blazer. As one can of insect spray emptied Stump grabbed another and continued the onslaught of bee killer that was keeping me from further attack. We returned to Gram's house.

"Gimmee the twenty dollar bill," she said. Stump handed it over. "Now," she said, "Go to Horner Road and get my water. And then fill my gas tank with your money when you get back to town."

"That's not fair." Steve said.

"If you prefer, I will tell your dad and grampa on you," she admonished Stump and then looked at me, "And I will tell your father too."

"I will buy the gas," I said to Stump as we got in the Blazer. I definitely did not want my father involved in this. I would have received punishment because Stump tried to get the wrong spring water, I just knew it. We returned with the water and went to the clubhouse around dark to fix the ruts. We were shoveling the gravel and raking it level when Dick, a club member, pulled in. The parking lot had some minor ruts in it before, but nothing like the ones we made. Dick had arrived to feed the beagles that he and some other members kept year round at the club kennels. They took turns feeding and cleaning the dogs. By the time he arrived the parking lot looked great, in fact it hadn't looked that good since the gravel was delivered several years previous. Dick was a distant relative to me on my mother's side. He walked up to me and said, "You

53

guys are pretty good kids. Lots of guys your age would be out looking for trouble at sunset. Yinz are fixing the parking lot." He gave me a congratulatory slap on the back. Pain surged across my body and tears began to well up within my eyes. I choked them back. "No need to get emotional," he said, "Take the compliment." He walked towards the kennels whistling with the impression that good boys still existed.

SPRINT TO THE END

Foot is a favorite conversation topic amongst beaglers. In this case foot is the colloquial term used to gauge speed. How fast is your dog? That dog is too slow. That dog is too loose! I, for one, measure the speed of a hound in terms of minutes/circle as it chases solo. I know, dogs will speed up when they are in a pack, but any hound unable to circle a rabbit without help has very little, maybe nothing, to offer the pack. That being said, who does not like the sound of a hound or a pack of beagles pounding a rabbit through a valley with the baying bouncing off the hills? Still, a solo beagle has to prove its mettle, and it is a joy to watch a hound that is fast and keeps the rabbit moving with very few breakdowns.

My father was very fleet afoot. When he was discharged from the Seabees after WWII he weighed 220 pounds, stood 6'2" and wore pants with a 31 inch waistline with a 34 inch inseam. He had the physique that you hope a judge might have at a trial—long and lean and able to run. As it is, we sometimes go to field trials and the judges refuse meals due to the rigors of running, but you wonder how they ever see any hound work, given the bulkiness of the guys. My dad never judged, He was too busy Working all the overtime he could get and pleasure running his hunting hounds instead of traveling the field trial circuit.

Dad was 45 when I was born. He was in his late 50's when I got my first beagle. He owned beagles in the 1950's, after the war, but had not owned any for a couple decades by the time I had to have a hunting dog. He shot a lot of rabbits in his youth because he would take risks close to roads, knowing that his long legs and fast stride could cut the dogs off before they reached the traffic. In his late 50's he was still quite fast, but was no longer as brave when it came to hunting those highway bunnies.

How fast do I run? Well, let's put it this way—not very. I still remember being a benchwarmer on a peewee football team. I was a backup linebacker. I ran with the linemen during sprints. I often finished well, but only because I had fast reflexes. The coach moved me to run with the running backs and ends, hoping I might show promise. I still remember his evaluation of my performance when I ran with the fast guys. Coach asked me "How can someone have such a massive lead at ten yards and then finish last by such a huge margin at 40 yards?"

I should add that my father was always working, and he had a steady stream of exhaust—from his pipe. When he first developed bladder cancer he changed from cigarettes to the pipe, hoping it would be healthier. I am not sure that is the case when you inhale the pipe smoke! When my first beagles were starting to hit their good hunting years, dad was 60. He had some breathing trouble from a lifetime of smoking—there were no tobacco warnings when he was a kid during the Great Depression. Even with damaged lungs he could run like the wind for short sprints.

As he aged he stayed trim. He was a healthy 185 pounds. I still remember when he lost his bladder to cancer. The local doctor kept burning out little tumors for years. Finally he said we had to go to a specialist in Buffalo, at the famous Roswell Cancer Institute. A hospital employee showed us a wall with portraits of all the famous people who sought treatment there. I remember there was a picture of John Wayne.

"You see sir," the employee said, "People who could go anywhere for their treatment come here."

"Yeah," Dad said looking at the young woman and then the picture of the Duke himself, "You know a lot of these people are dead, right?"

The doctors are top notch there, however. I remember the surgeon saying, "I wish you had come here sooner, we could have done more. As it is you will lose the bladder and the cancer may return."

"My urologist in Pennsylvania never gave me the option to come here until now," Dad said.

"You may have made him a better doctor, at the expense of your bladder." The surgeon said, "Say, I am looking at your medical records here, how far are you from the place in Pennsylvania where they brew Straub's Beer."

"Not far," Dad said, "Why?"

"I like to have a beer at night," the surgeon said, "Could you bring me a bottle or two to try?"

"On the day of the surgery I walked into the Roswell Cancer Institute carting a case of Straub beer, in the brown bottles. If you ask the people from northwest PA what they like better—the green bottles of Straub or the brown, they will fight about it. I don't know why, it is the same beer. It was a long walk to the surgical floor, and it was early in the morning. Dad did not like Straub beer, so he was not going to drink 22 of them just to give the doctor two bottles. The surgeon was getting a case!

"This is for the Doc doing my dad's operation," I said to the nurse at the check in counter.

"OH," her eyes got large, "Umm, I don't think I can--"

"He asked us to bring it." Dad said. She probably thought we were real hillbillies bringing a case of beer— sort of like paying the old country doctor with chickens. The surgery was a success and dad was home soon, albeit on chemotherapy. On a follow up visit the surgeon asked my father if he had any questions.

"Yeah, he said, years ago I struggled to keep a heavy machine from falling on my feet at work when the other guy dropped his end. It was several hundred pounds and I slumped down to the ground and let it rest on my body until help came. I did not want to break a foot—I would have missed way too much work with a broken foot—or two broken feet. I have a bad hernia from the incident, and it isn't bulging out now like it used to."

"Nope, Mr. Ford the doctor said, "You can quit wearing that hernia belt."

"Oh?"

"Yessir, I fixed it while I was removing your bladder."

"None of my paperwork mentions it?" Dad said.

"I didn't bill you for it. That procedure cost exactly one case of beer."

There were follow ups that showed dad to be cancer free. The visits were every month, then every six months, then every year. No problems. The drawback, of course, to not having your bladder is the fact that you must wear an artificial one on your side. The capacity of this bladder is smaller than the one that the Good Lord gave us, and so the contents must be emptied more often. The complications for hunting mostly involve ensuring that the thickets and briars do not tear the plastic bladder. Dad always wore a cotton duck brush shirt and pants when running dogs, even in the summer. I often would wear sneakers, blue jeans, and a tee shirt, especially in the beagle club, where there were ample opportunities to catch dogs on a mowed path, thus avoiding briars altogether.

Even so, I still recall a chase where the dogs went out towards the back end of the running grounds and their voices became more faint.

"Where are they?" I said.

"I can't hear them!" Dad answered.

"I can barely hear them."

Dad tapped out his pipe and started sprinting. I am embarrassed to say that he could outrun me at over 60 years of age—at least for the first 100 yards. He ran a mile at just over 4:20 as a young man, and said he was a sprinter more so than a distance runner. The back end of the running grounds were not maintained as well, and the brush was thick. The fence appeared to be fine, but there must have been a hole under it. Later that week I found the hole and fixed it. Dad vaulted the fence, careful to jump so that he did not hook the bladder on the wire. I jumped the fence and then finally passed dad, I yelled "DOWN!" and the male lowered to the ground. Princess was ahead of him and kept going. I leashed Duke and saw my father slipping between the trees, catching Princess out on the road. He was out of breath for quite some time, but a fast quarter mile was still in my dad. Whereas an asthmatic might reach for a medical inhaler after such exertion, he lit his pipe and filled the air with apple scented tobacco.

I can also tell you that in his sixties he humored his son's love to hunt the PA snowshoe hare, and would run long distances along Allegheny ridges of hemlock and mountain laurel handling dogs while I stood statue still, waiting for the elusive white ghosts to appear. After I shot my limit (two per day then) he would then hunt a hare, if there was time. We often shot more cottontails than hare on those days afield.

Dad loved baseball. He was a big Reds fan, or more accurately a Pete Rose fan. Reds fans are a rare thing in Pennsylvania, and father would sit out in the yard at night and tune in the a.m. radio to listen to the Cincinnati games. The radio had an orange glow as it cackled and hissed, and dad's pipe had a brighter orange glow as he puffed nervously in the late innings. We went to a few games in Pittsburgh over the years, and we were some of the very few cheering for the Reds in the Steel City! I remember the summer before I went to college, Dad wanted to see one more Red's game, but was cautious because he did not want to stop the car every 45 minutes to empty the bladder.

"We can drive straight through," I said, after getting home from my summer job, which consisted of holding a sign for the Department of Transportation while maintenance was performed on the roads.

"How?" he asked.

"I already drilled a hole through the floor board of the truck," I said, "You can use that hose that you hook up to at night, the one that drains into that large jug."

He gave me that look of wary optimism that he was famous for, "Really?" He asked.

"Yep, and a rubber stopper that is made for a chemistry test tube to plug the hole in the floor and put the plastic tubing through," I said, "Only you won't have a large container in the truck to worry about. You can Pee all the way to Pittsburgh."

"I can disconnect from it when we park!" He beamed.

"Ah, I dunno." His optimistic look faded into his worried one.

"I bought tickets close to a bathroom, I called and asked about that. You can even have a beer and make it to the restroom easy."

"You already bought the tickets?"

"Yep, we are going. Happy Father's Day."

And so we did, he emptied coffee along PA route 28 going to the game, and he emptied a beer on the same highway as we returned home. The Reds won too. A few days later Dad and I were sitting on the porch after having just returned from running the dogs in the evening. Scooter Shott was walking down the street past our house. "Hi Harold," he said as he passed.

"Hello Scooter," father replied. Scooter shuffled past us, limping hard on both legs.

Dad looked at me, "Did you know he played semi-professional football for a team called the Shamrocks?"

I looked at Scooter who was moving quickly, but definitely limping, "No, I didn't know that."

"Yep," Dad said, "He was the only guy in school that ever beat me in a footrace."

"I bet he was fast to play football like that," I answered.

"Yeah," father said, all of us unaware that his cancer was about to return and that he would be dead in just over a year, "But my knees never took the pounding his did, and I'd race his ass right now!" He did sprint to the end. Happy Father's Day

WALKING AROUND MONEY

Walking around money is an important thing. I got my first walking around money when I was 11 years old and took over the *Erie Sunday Times* paper route. The paper was sufficiently far away from our town that it never covered news from our area. The popularity was rooted in the fact that the Sunday coupons section was as thick as the comics. My wife will often create a grocery list and send me to the store to get said items. Actually, she now text messages me the litany of food. Then she sends another text message that says, "If you want to eat supper tonight, it would be nice if you got these things on the way home—if you have time."

Notice that she is not ordering me to get the groceries. And she gives me a way out of it because it says that I can get those things if I have time. But the whole text is premised on wifely power that says, and I am adding the emphasis here, "*IF YOU WANT TO EAT SUPPER TONIGHT.*" Naturally, I want to eat supper every night, so I get the items on the list. I can guess right away what we are eating by the list. Ground beef, tomato sauce, pasta, garlic, onions, lettuce, and hot sausage links is easy to identify: pasta with meat sauce, salad, and hot sausage on the side for the kid and me. If she doesn't specify the pasta I always get ravioli. I grew up in a German-American home and did not get to eat much pasta, so I look forward to that dish.

My youth was characterized by a culture where the menu could never be guessed by looking in the shopping cart. Women, including my mother, would enter the grocery stores with amazing quantities of coupons in their hands. Sometimes they sat the small child in the top-seat section of the cart and made the kid hold the coupons. Have you ever wondered if we really want to put our fruit where someone's kid was sitting in a dirty diaper an hour ago? I digress. Anyway, the cart was filled with whatever was on sale, and in particular whatever was advertised as "buy one get one free." I have seen shrewd women fill an entire cart and pay very little money at the end. Once I saw the store manager called over to the cashier because when everything was calculated the store owed the shopper money. The woman was drummed out of the grocery store like a card counter in Vegas.

These coupons were the key to my walking around money because they caused the paper to sell itself. Carrying 150 Sunday papers with eleven year old muscles presents its own problems, but I was thrilled. Every year I took Christmas tips to Grice's Gun Store in Clearfield. It was a pretty far drive south, but it was well known as a big gun store even then. My dad would legally buy the guns, but I was proud as a peacock when paying for the gun with my own money. I told my wife that the only people who had more one dollar bills than me were waiters and waitresses. She added, "Or dancers." I did not inquire as to how she gleaned that knowledge—maybe I don't want to know. Anyway, I bought my first side by side double barrel shotgun at Grice's. It was a heavy, cheap, 20 gauge. That was the last year I had the route after 6 years. My first pup was purchased from profits earned on the same route.

At the age of eleven, I was a little young for a paperboy, but I was ambitious. Kids no longer go outside, and if Children and Youth Services saw a kid carrying a sack of newspapers the parents would be questioned for breaking child labor laws. I never see youngsters riding bicycles at all, let alone with a news paper sack tied to the handle bars and one across each shoulder. Most paperboys are currently retired guys who deliver the news by automobile. My hunch is that these old timers need walking around money. Walking around money gets rare when you are married. It becomes extinct when you are raising a teenager. My walking around money once came from change. When I was single, I would dump all my change into a big plastic container. When it was full I had enough money for a nice toy—a tracking collar, a dog box, maybe a gun. It was a big container.

Do you remember that day about 6th grade when the school took all the girls away to a room to learn the facts of life while the boys were left to play dodge ball in the gym? One of the things that I am sure the girls learned was how to hoard change when they became brides. I haven't seen a substantial quantity of quarters, nickels, or dimes since I said my vows. The ash tray in my truck once held enough quarters to cover parking and buy a tank of gas in case of an emergency. Currently, my ash tray has a few pennies and those rubber bands made of fabric utilized by women to tie their hair into a ponytail.

I accept the loss of change as something akin to a marital tax. It is even easier than taxes, as there is no need to mail the money to a government agency. The chief financial officer of the matrimonial government authority just comes and takes the money. You don't even realize how much is missing, which eases the pain. The payments aren't quarterly, they are haphazard. The way it works is simple. You wake up and take a shower and brush your teeth. Following this you get dressed. While doing so you look at your coin container on the dresser and you notice that its contents are less today than the last time you remember looking at it. Mostly you see pennies. You smile happily, feeling that proud sense of accomplishment that you get when you file your taxes a week early or pay a bill. Off to work you go to generate more change...

Walking around money now comes less frequent, but it is there. If you are careful you can find a safe place to hide change. Better yet, find several places to hide the coins. I think this is what financial experts mean by diversifying your funds. Find places your chief financial officer doesn't like to go. Dog kennels are good. Basements work fine. Anyplace near a large collection of sharp fishing hooks is usually safe. Just make sure you leave enough in the official jar for the matrimonial government authority to take it. The amount she takes isn't as important as you think. All that is necessary is that she feels you are being prevented from wasting your money on nonessential hunting supplies. If you are real bold you can try to take change back from the chief financial officer's purse. This can yield high rewards, but all high yield investments are accompanied by high risk. As any man who has ever picked up a purse knows, the damn things are heavier than they look—unnaturally heavy. I mean heavy like the beaker full of mercury next to the same sized beaker full of water in high school science glass.

Change accumulates in a purse. This is because it is near impossible to reach the bottom of a purse due to all the other items. There is not sufficient room for a hand to squeeze to the bottom. Remember that day in 6th grade when you were left in the gym? Girls also learned how to violate the laws of physics and have more than one piece of matter occupy the same space. If you have ever heard these words, "Honey, would you get the pen out of my purse?" you are aware of the complexities of unpacking a purse. Stuff just keeps coming out of the thing. The pen does, in fact, exist in there. But it is in the substrata, beneath receipts, chewing gum, breath mints, makeup, backup jewelry, and a hair dryer. Do not try to repack the purse. You do not have the skills, you were playing dodge ball, remember? Just go out to the shed and get three bushel baskets to contain the contents and apologize for not being able to pack the thing. She will appreciate your efforts. At this point get the coins. There could be as much as 50 dollars in there. In the overall scheme of things she will never notice such a minimal difference in weight. A Himalayan Sherpa who routinely summits Everest would crumple under the weight of a married woman's purse. Leave the pennies to ease your getaway.

Now you can afford a trial or two. Maybe you could buy an extra tracking collar. A collapsible water bowl to carry in the field for your dogs is nice too. Long term investing is an option as well. You can save the money and put it in the bank. By this, I mean you could buy a gun. I will be the first to admit that I have a problem. That is the first step, they say, in getting help. I love old American made side by side shotguns. The sad thing is that gun shops know it. Just the other day I was driving to do a hospital visit when my cell phone rang, "Hello?"

"Bob, this is John at Lion Country Supply, how are ya?"

"Good, how about you?"

"Fine, fine. Hey, I just got a 12 gauge Double Barrel Lefever in, and I thought of you. It's in good shape too. Just wanted to let you know. It should be here for awhile before it gets sold, but I wanted to tell ya about it."

You know you are an addict when the dealer calls you upon the arrival of the "good stuff." I tried to forget the call, but a few days later I checked my change stashes after the chief financial officer went to bed. The ground is hard to dig in February. Then I had a birthday and received some gifts of paper money. After being married this long, I almost forgot what paper money looked like. I was getting closer to the amount needed to get the gun. Soon afterward I was asked to fetch a computer flash drive from the chief financial officer's purse, and...

"Hi Bob," John said as I walked into Lion Country Supply. He handed me the Lefever. The cost was reasonable. For just a bit more money they had a used side by side 28 gauge. I did not own any 28 gauges. The gun is very light, and delivers the same punch as a 20. It isn't American made, but it is very nice. I am putting the gun in the bank vault, also known as the gun safe. There is room in there now that the coins have been removed. Make sure the chief financial officer doesn't know the combination to the vault.

TREEING

It is no secret that Advent and Lent are busy times in the church. Advent has many activities that make the month before Christmas a blur. There is, of course, the decorating of the church. In addition to wreaths, holly, ivy, and poinsettias, this season also involves the calculated cutting of the biggest tree you can possibly stuff into the corner of the sanctuary. Often a tree that looks impressive in the woods is only a mediocre specimen when placed in a room with a twenty foot high ceiling. A behemoth of a tree that fills the corner nicely also requires all sorts of gravity defying innovations to prevent the festive evergreen from tumbling over onto a worshiping congregation. One of my great fears is that the complex rigging of bailing wire and eye hooks will fail catastrophically, resulting in a third of the congregation being covered with tinsel and the tell tale scratches of evergreen needles. I am something of an expert on evergreen scratches, as I often hunt rabbits in such cover. I have never liked using gloves while shooting, and so unless the air is temperature is below twenty degrees with an additional wind chill to match, I tend to hunt the pines (or any other cover) with bare hands even in the winter, and I am always self-conscious about the red scratches that cover the backs of my hands from pine needles, greenbrier, and multi-floral rose. My hands look bad in hunting season, almost diseased.

Another perpetual fear is that the washtub that serves as a tree stand for the holidays will develop a leak. When you put a massive blue spruce into a 35 gallon galvanize wash tub, there is always anxiety. Sure, the tub is designed to hold water, but the tree is wedged into the tub as tightly as possible using a couple of two-by-fours that are attached to the bottom of the giant blue spruce's trunk, screwed into the bottom in an X pattern. As if the giant X base did not strain the washtub's structural integrity enough, the entire tree stand is then filled with gravel in order to weigh it down. Even after all of this, the tub seems to hold a tremendous volume of water. While there is a plastic tarp under the washtub, I am not sure how that would be much help in the event that the tub developed a leak.

Each year we test the tub for such a leak. The proper way to do this would be to fill the tub with water and let it sit someplace for a few days, where any seeping moisture could be detected readily. But, no, the way we always test the bucket is to fill it with water on the day we get the tree and have two guys hold it in the air, so that two other men can stand with their hands in their pockets and stare at the ground looking for drops of falling water.

"UMPH," one of the parishioners holding the tub says as he develops a hernia, "Is it leaking?"

"Nope," Another shakes his head as he bends at the waist to look underneath the tub. And with that, the tub is approved for another year of duty. I spend the next four weeks in a panic, as I have seen small children condemned by church trustees for spilling juice on a carpet that was NOT in the sanctuary. I can only imagine the penalties that would be dispensed for the soiling of the sanctuary carpet with muddy tree water. It is always a good idea to have several trustees on the team of people who erect the Christmas tree—they tend to be less vicious when they are partially culpable.

In addition to all of the church activities, there is also the reality of the rifle season for white-tail deer in Pennsylvania. This tends to fall mostly, or entirely, within Advent. It is two weeks long and begins the Monday after Thanksgiving. In fact, I know of no school that is actually open in Pennsylvania on the Monday after Thanksgiving. I am sure that there are kids in cities somewhere that are off school that day and have no idea why. The school boards there may not remember the rationale, and they have forgotten that they once had hunting traditions in their culture. They probably call the day "Thanksgiving Monday" and are happy enough to extend the long weekend, oblivious to the buck fever griping the countryside.

The beagles are generally tired at this time of year, because it marks the end of the first small game season. I like to hunt deer in places where I run beagles on rabbits. I call this policy "Taking out the trash." Running deer is one of the worst sins a beagle can commit, and the act of chasing any unwanted game is called trash running by houndsmen. Thus, Taking out the trash is the act of shooting a deer where I hunt rabbits or train beagles. My wife says that it is the only week of the year when I am actually good at taking out the trash. I get my doe tag just for the purpose of removing hooved temptations from my running grounds. Sure, whacking a doe seems too easy and unchallenging, but catching a young beagle as it chases a deer up a hill that is virtually a sheer cliff is beyond challenging. My goal is to always train beagles in cover that has more rabbits than deer! I would never claim that my dogs never chased a deer, but keeping them in cover that has lots of bunnies is the best way to break the bad habit for me.

Processing deer is another concern. My garage adjoins the house, and the floor is lined with plastic whenever a deer needs butchered. Have you ever tried to keep a garage surgically clean? We do. I don't want even one scrap of hide or scent pad within the sniffing range of the beagles that are in the house. The hounds, of course, are keenly interested in what I am doing, and I have a strict no-odor zone rule when it comes to the clothing worn while processing venison. I leave the cold garage after the steaks and roasts are neatly placed into a cooler, and then go straight into the basement and place all the clothing into the washing machine. At this point I proceed directly to the adjoining bathroom and wash the deer scent away with a hot shower. To be accurate, I should say that I take a shower that alternates between scolding hot and frigid, since I always forget to wash the clothes in cold water and I am a victim of the various cycles of the washing machine as it de-scents my clothes whilst I shower.

The hunting house beagles have been in lockdown throughout this process. I place dog crates in my bedroom and confine them until the meat is in the freezer and the garage, kitchen, and deer-scented laundry is cleaned. No doubt the beasts are under the impression that they are being punished, but the reality is I am trying to keep them from temptation. Most of my hunting companions are primarily, or exclusively, interested in deer hunting. I look at deer season as a chance to improve my rabbit grounds and put some meat in the freezer. I would rather be rabbit hunting, and many people do not understand this odd characteristic that afflicts beaglers.

I think I have always been this way too, dating back to my first beagles as a kid. There was nothing that bothered me more than events interrupting my time in the field with the beagles. When I was kid (way back in the 1900's, as my kid says) a hunter was only allowed one deer per year in Pennsylvania. There were two weeks of buck season, and two days of doe season. I shot the first legal buck I could get, and a spike buck was legal at that time in my home state.

"You killed a spike?" a friend might ask.

"It's an Allegheny National Forest eleven point," I would correct them.

"It's a spike!" my friend would tease.

"It's an eleven point!" I would defend myself, "This right side has one point, and the left side has one point. A one and another one make an eleven." Math was easy for me, as you can see.

I loved ending deer season early, because it allowed me to take the hounds to the Beagle Club and get them in shape for the second small game season, which began after Christmas. It was also after Christmas that our small varying hare season happened. I was constantly asking deer hunters if they saw any varying hare tracks or an actual hare. Just as soon as deer season ended I was out in the thickets and mountain laurel looking for hare. Hemlock stands were my favorite places to find the tracks. Daylight is a limited commodity in mid-December. By the time a kid gets home from school and changes clothes, it is really hard to do much scouting before the sun sets.

Mid-December is also the season for what we called "treeing." Treeing begins in the weeks leading up to Christmas, and it is the act of going to look at your family and friends' trees. Likewise, at some point, these same

people came and looked at your Christmas tree.
Ostensibly the purpose of treeing was to visit one another,
but the ulterior motive was to compare the quality of your
snacks and beverages with that of other people's.

"Boy, if they cut that pepperoni any smaller it would
have gotten stuck in your tooth and you couldn't eat it,"
would be a typical complaint about the food served at a
house you just visited. On the opposite end of the
spectrum was a condemnation that went something like,
"Who the hell do they think they are serving shrimp? John
D. RockeFord?" my dad once said about a relative on the
Ford side that provided a rather lavish spread for company.
This brings up another component of treeing—it is better to
be one of the first houses to host a gathering, as the
snacks tended to get bigger and more expensive as advent
progresses. Nothing says peace on earth and good will to
the poor quite like escalating buffets of cheese, meat, and
nuts.

The one exception to this tendency towards decadence
in food was the fruitcake. Every home provided fruitcake
as the dessert portion of the evening. I am not sure why,
as I cannot think of a single person who would voluntarily
eat fruitcake without the peer pressure that accompanies
holiday gatherings. Maybe the alcoholic drinks made
them forget how nasty fruitcake tastes. Refusing the
fruitcake would be like telling a little kid you refused to
have a piece of their birthday cake—sure, you could do
that, buy it would be a major breach in social convention.
How do I know that it is a breach of social protocol? I
know because I broke it.

"Bob, do you want a piece of Gramma's fruitcake?" I
was asked. Actually, I wasn't being asked per se, since the
question was delivered while thrusting a slice of fruitcake
into my hands. I was being ordered with a request. I
grabbed the plate with one hand and was amazed at the
weight of it. It defied the mind. It was like science class
when the teacher put a container of water next to an
equivalent volume of liquid mercury—heavy as a woman's
purse, in other words. Gram's fruitcake was beyond
dense. It was served on a real plate, as opposed to paper,
because the paper plate lacked the rigidity necessary to

hold it in one hand, it was like holding the dessert in a paper towel.

"Couldn't I have some liver and inions instead?" was my response, everyone knew I despised liver and onions. It is worth noting that this was in the days of corporal punishment (you know, back in the 1900's) and my father immediately lifted me off the ground with a swift foot to my hindquarters. Because of that, it hurt to sit on my hindquarters for a few hours, which was convenient because the adults sat at the table while the kids stood and ate their fruitcake on the counter top in the kitchen. Standing eased the sting in my back side. You almost couldn't put enough butter on my grandmother's fruitcake. No one would say, "This is really dry," as that would be rude. Instead we all slathered butter on our fruitcake to provide enough lubricant to get the stuff to slide down our throats. In case you didn't know, buttering fruitcake is never done—but you may want to try it, if your Gram bakes a fruitcake like mine did. All fruitcake batter looks like cement mix, packed full of dried fruit instead of gravel. The fruit never seems to rehydrate. My grandmother's cake was most difficult to chew. I once bit into a dried apricot that was harder than a cough drop. Peanut brittle must have been softer.

Treeing was mandatory, and I despised missing my hare scouting operations just to look at a tree that contained the exact same decorations that it did last year. More than that, the tree sat in the exact same corner, and if it was an artificial tree it was the exact same tree! Alas, all it took was my returning from the woods late on one occasion to invoke the wrath of family law, and I was forbidden from scouting on days when an evening treeing event was planned. I would comply, but was not happy to go visiting. Hare season was only a little over a week long and the daily limit was two (The season is shorter now, and the daily limit is one). Treeing still has a bit of a negative connotation to me now. Especially when it happens after Christmas and people leave their presents under the tree for company to see. At that point the purpose seems to be about comparing Christmas budgets. Again, there is no good news on earth to be found in that practice.

I still do not get to spend time in the woods before Christmas, but that is because of work. Kids programs, caroling, cantatas, and other functions can consume a lot of time in December. But that is OK with me. I no longer care about hunting hare on December 26th the way I did as a kid. Sure, I will go look for snow shoe hare, but if I cannot locate any to hunt I will live with it. The reason I do not care is because I now love to go on one treeing visit each year. My wife is from the Adirondacks, and we take the seven and a half hour trek to her parents' house every year. My mother-in-law makes fruitcake, but I have the advantage of house beagles. I always take one or two beagles with me to see the in-laws. A beagle lying at one's feet can help dispatch a slice of fruitcake with minimal effort. All it takes is enough patience to wait until everyone is straining their hand muscles trying to cut their slab of the dry dessert with a fork. At that point you simply rip off a hunk of your own fruitcake (it is like cement, it will fracture along its internal fault lines) and quickly hand it to the beagle under the table. Nothing pleases a host more than asking for a second piece of fruitcake. Don't ask for a third, because that would just be ludicrous—no one could eat three slabs! The beagle always appreciates both desserts, and then wanders off to food-coma in a corner. I amazed that the little dog can carry the weight of two fruitcake slices, but the beagle is a remarkable breed. Besides, he will need the energy from that cake—because the Adirondacks have more hare than you can imagine, and the daily limit is six. No scouting necessary in the cedar swamp that I hunt! Merry Christmas.

CHRISTMAS TREES AND SHOPPING

One of the great advantages of marriage is that when it comes to holiday gifts I only have to shop for my wife. This is true for friends' birthdays, anniversaries, weddings or even Christmas. Now, I might point out that I am indeed lucky on this issue—as Renee is the kind of person that can shop all day and only spend $20. Early in our marriage she realized that my tolerance for accompanying her in shopping centers was quite limited.

"Don't you sit on a deer stand for 8 hours at a time?" she asked.

"Yes."

"In cold air?" she continued her examination.

"Bitterly so, at times."

"And yet sitting on the bench by the water fountain in this warm mall is too difficult?" she sighed through pursed lips. It is not easy to sigh through pursed lips without making a sound that resembles flatulence.

"Yes!" I leaped for joy, "Now you understand."

"No, I don't understand at all!" she threw her hands in the air in obvious disgust.

And she doesn't. It is the crowds of people, the yelling and bickering that shopping apparently induces in people, and the overwhelming sense that I am the only person in the entire building who doesn't know what clothes the famous actors wear. I don't even know the names of many actors. More than that, most of the people are walking around while pressing buttons on their cell phones and staring at the screen. Some of them walk into me, despite the fact that I am sitting on a bench so close to the waterfall that a few backsplash sprinkles occasionally land on my head. This is all exaggerated at Christmas time, when people go crazy about shopping, going so far as to awake on the Friday after Thanksgiving at an hour when raccoon hunters are just getting ready to come home. This is Good Friday for shoppers.

Remember when that Wal-Mart had a person trampled to death when they unlocked the doors? Out of respect, they did close the store for a few hours. Sheesh. When I was a kid a lady broke another woman's arm fighting for a cabbage patch doll. All of this seems detrimental to the Spirit of Christmas, but I am just a clergyman. Madison Avenue has the corner on the holiday. And the credit card companies.

Nope, I let Renee go shopping alone, and she buys for everyone—except herself. That is my job. I used to by her something on Christmas Eve. It was easier to do it that way—the stores were so low on stuff that it drastically cut back on the choices, thus speeding up the shopping time. A full inventory of merchandise might result in my shopping for upwards of 4 minutes. Curtailed Christmas Eve stockpiles can get me out of the store in less than 2 minutes, so long as the clerk knows how to make change, since I am the last person in the world, apparently, who uses cash. I am told that such efficiency rivals that of bank robbers, who are really time conscious about their work. I think I could shop even faster, if I had a gun. It might, however, be poor form to wave around a handgun saying, "I wanna buy a necklace and leave this place right now!" I doubt the police officers would accept disdain of shopping as a reasonable excuse for cutting the line at the store with a firearm.

It turns out that the leftover goodies that stores still have remaining on the day before Christ's birthday are not the best selections—they are like the inhabitants of the Island of Misfit Toys from the *Rudolph* special. Except instead of being cute, the items in the department stores are, and I quote this directly from my wife, "Tacky." I find this hard to believe, given the fact that most of her ear rings are the size, and color (very bright) of bass lures. I did not think she found anything to be tacky—she married me, for crying out loud. So I decided to shop online for the past few years. To be honest, I was lost. I had no idea what to get her. I just sat there looking at the amazon.com screen. So I called other women, and asked them what they wanted for Christmas.

"Oh Pastor, you don't have to get me anything," was a common response to my line of questioning.

"I'm not," I would answer, "But I have no idea what to get my wife. Is cash too impersonal?"

Apparently it is, unless it is a large amount of cash, and then it is seen as acceptable. So I would get ideas from these women about what they wanted to receive from their husbands. I would then tell their husbands. These wives were thrilled with their gifts. My wife was not as pleased. Perhaps the dilemma was that nothing I got her resembled a bass lure. Now, I am here to save all the men out there who are both hunters and married—or a have a long term girlfriend. Hopefully you do not have a marriage and a long-term girlfriend. That would be a sin. And expensive at Christmas, I would think. Here is the answer to your problems—catalogs. All you have to do is buy some hunting supplies from a few catalog companies. You will then start receiving catalogs from stores you never knew existed. I receive enough catalogs in the mail every day to heat a small cabin for an entire year. Look through them for unique gifts. Hammacher Schlemmer (I never heard of them either) sends me catalogs all the time. Last year I bought a bathroom towel warmer for my wife. I saw it advertised, and I thought, "My wife always complains about how cold she is when she gets out of the shower."

She is so cold that she is irrational about it. She actually believes that putting socks on cold feet will "keep the cold in." Naturally, this makes no sense, but such lack of basic scientific knowledge is tolerated in a person who can shop for 12 hours and only spend $20. She loved the towel warmer. One year I got her a gizmo from a catalog that supposedly killed germs on her cell phone. I have no idea if it works or not. Neither does she (remember, she thinks socks keep your feet cold). My recent Christmas gifts have all been big hits. Now, here is the real payoff in all of this—while your wife is shopping for every other relative in your collective families, you can go rabbit hunting! Saturdays are perfect—we wake up together, eat breakfast together, and then get ready for the hunt. I put on boots and insulated clothes to hunt bunnies, she puts on walking sneakers, comfortable clothes, and bass lures to hunt bargains.

At the end of the day I return with a couple rabbits and tired beagles. She returns with $20 of perfectly chosen gifts, or several $20 gifts. She is also as tired as the beagles, since she probably walked twice as far as they ran. She will compare the prices on any given item in 2-19 different stores before buying it. If I were to throw a GPS collar in her purse, I am sure that the data would show that her average speed was slower than the hounds, but she would no doubt cover way more ground than the pooches. When she is shopping she runs check free. By that I mean that she does not lose her quarry even temporarily. Or use a checkbook—she is a debit card kind of shopper.

Her willingness to pursue bargains also gives me time to find the perfect Christmas tree. Now there are several tree farms that have given me permission to hunt on their Christmas tree plantations anytime I want—except for the time period between Thanksgiving and Orthodox Christmas. Orthodox Christians, for those who don't know, celebrate Christmas on January 7th. Sure, there are historical reasons to explain this, but the key detail here is that an Orthodox husband can get a really nice item for his wife on January 6 for cheap. After Christmas sales are where the real savings are, and the necklace that I could not afford on Dec. 24th is priced to move by Jan 6—the other Christmas Eve.

Where was I? Oh, yes, trees. I am not allowed to shoot rabbits in the tree farms until after Jan7. Apparently shotguns are not the mood music that farmers are looking for when families are strolling through the Christmas tree farms looking for the perfect conifer to adorn the corner of their living room. Barking beagles on a sight chase do not exactly reinforce the image of a lion and lamb lying down together in peace and harmony.

I tend to get my tree in the wild. A wild tree is heartier, or at least I think so. Any tree that is able to grow into a perfect shape without the benefit of pruning is a better specimen. The other benefit of a wild tree is that they are very deceptive in size. A tree farmer could tell you how tall a tree stands. "That's a six-footer," the farmer might say. If you are admiring a particularly full tree, the same farmer can caution you, "Now you will need at least a ten foot ceiling for that particular tree." This kind of information—the height of the tree—really limits your selection. I like to choose my tree while hunting rabbits. As December nears I will have chosen the perfect evergreen. The perfect tree, of course, is a blue spruce. A Blue Spruce is the most gorgeous of all festive trees, as far as I am concerned. There is only one drawback to this evergreen—it has needles that could be used for sewing leather dog leashes together. A barefoot always seems to find these needles. A socked foot is even worse, as the needle hides in the sock and jabs you periodically. Removing the sock seldom results in finding the needle. Apparently socks keep needles and cold air close to the foot.

One fine day last December I managed to shoot my daily limit pretty early in the morning. The dogs were chasing another rabbit, and I decided to let them have fun while I went to cut down the Blue Spruce that I had been admiring for several Saturdays. I put the rabbits in the bed of the truck and grabbed a hack saw from the tool box. The trunk of this amazing tree was, in fact, smaller in diameter than my thigh, despite what my wife says. I have small thighs, too, by the way. It was, however, a tall tree. A large chunk of the tree stuck out of the bed of my truck. The needles had maimed my arms in the process of felling, dragging, and loading the behemoth into my truck. In fact, my arms and hands looked as if they had been covered in tiny red dots of paint. It resembled some sort of rash, or maybe a medieval plague. But the tree was perfect. I had to take the dog box out of my truck and let the dogs ride in the cab with me. Hey, I like to *Windex* the windows once in a while. Wet beagle noses leave a very distinctive smudge.

Lenny had to loan me a chainsaw when I got home. This is because the tree was way too tall for our house. Also, my chainsaw did not start. Anyone who has ever owned a chainsaw knows that the only thing that fails to start more frequently than a chainsaw is a weed whacker. Unless you trim weeds every day or cut trees for a living,

both of these tools are near impossible to start. Lenny
came over with his big chainsaw.

"Whadya need this thing for?" He asked as he came to
the front door. I took him around back, where a massive
Blue Spruce lay partially in the house, mostly in the yard.

"Think we can take care of this before my wife spends
$20 and comes home from shopping?" I asked.

"Good God man!" Lenny shrieked, "A wife could spend
that getting a mookoo chooka abbago mocha coffee thingy
on the way to the store!"

"Nah," I reassured him, "We probably have another
hour, maybe two. She won't shoot the first sale she sees.
She is a trophy hunter."

When we got done we had the tree in the corner of the
living room. It was pared down to 8 feet tall, barely
scraping the ceiling. It was good for hanging lots of
decorations, as it was about 6 feet in diameter, roughly. I
thought it was the perfect solution to the vacant corner
that had been bothering my wife, who thought we needed a
chair over there. Lenny took the rest of the tree home with
him to make a brush pile at the beagle club. There was
even enough room left amongst the giant limbs in his one
ton truck bed for the chainsaw, barely.

By the time you read this it will be December, and my
shopping will be finished. I may even have a tree selected,
if not decorated. I hope this is the last year I have to buy
my wife a present with the catalog. I started hunting
rabbits with an orthodox Christian. He goes Christmas
shopping every year around January 1 and gets great post-
Christmas specials. I think I will have him get my wife the
same thing he gets his wife, pay him for it, and then hide it
until next Christmas. Sound like a good plan? Who am I
kidding? The first time she runs a Blue Spruce needle
through her bare foot three months after the tree has left
the house I will have to give her the gift in order to get back
on her good-side. She won't even know that I perfected her
own game--$20 and zero hours shopping. Merry
Christmas.

BOW BUNNIES

"I don't like the look in your eye lately," my wife said to me, not many weeks ago.

"Whaddya mean," I asked, "Is it a mean look?"

"No."

"Do I look confused?" I took a second swing.

"Oh, definitely not," she answered.

"Is it a look of worry?"

"Nope," she shook her head signifying strike three. "You have an expensive look in your eye."

I have a few beagles in the house with rather extraordinary senses of smell, but my wife has a sixth sense when it comes to detecting my outdoor pursuits and how they might lead me to spending money. This most recent passion all started a few weeks ago when I went to ETAR, the Eastern Traditional Archery Rendezvous held each year outside Coudersport, PA. People come from everywhere to shoot 3D targets, buy stuff, and talk with other enthusiasts. Of course, the focus is on big game, and in particular whitetails.

I, myself, have been known to chase deer with a stick and string. Although, to be fair, it is with a stick made of high-tech materials with pulleys on the ends that allow the shooter to hold the arrow at full draw with little to no exertion. Did I mention the peep sights that make accurate shooting to 40 yards relatively simple? October is a good month to bow hunt for me, and I will often hunt the first few hours of daylight before taking the hounds to the beagle club. The club running grounds are full of rabbits, and the scenting conditions are not great by the time I get there at late morning. Chasing under such mediocre conditions makes the hounds run awesome when the rabbit season opens on the last Saturday of October; and they finally get to pound bunnies on morning dew. Typically I will let the hounds chase for an hour or two while I get my laptop out at the clubhouse and check my church emails and grade homework assignment for the introductory college classes that I teach. I will then put the hounds in the club kennels, use the clubhouse to change out of my brush pants and into some *Dockers*, and a dress shirt, and then go do hospital and nursing home visits. On the way home I retrieve the dogs. It is handy having a beagle club between my house and the city where most of my pastoral care visits happen. Once rabbit season opens, I cease archery hunting for deer and become a full-time houndsman chasing cottontails.

ETAR gave me the bug to go backwards in technology. In my home state of Pennsylvania, crossbows are the bow that most guys use now. My compound bow seemed very easy in comparison to a recurve, but the very sight of guys carrying scoped crossbows seems anathema to me! We need a scope to shoot 40 yards? Really? The guys at ETAR were shooting recurves, longbows, and other such traditional weapons. Of course, a lot of ETAR was about costumes too. There were a few longbow shooters dressed like Robin Hood. The occasional 19th century mountain man costume was seen. I even saw one guy in a Scottish Kilt—not sure if that was the best costume for avoiding ticks.

I watched these guys shooting as accurately—and usually more accurate—with a recurve than I could shoot with a compound bow. Time and time again they hit the kill zone of various and assorted three dimensional targets, and all of the kill zones were no bigger than...a rabbit. Enter the expensive look that my wife had noticed! I got the idea of trying to hunt cottontails with a recurve. You know, the bunnies that will on rare occasions stop in your field of sight as the dogs are behind them, sorting out a check? I want to shoot those rabbits with a recurve.

I dialed the chairman of our church's administrative council. "Walt, I said, do you have a recurve bow?"

"Yeah, I just had it re-strung. It is a *Bear Kodiak Magnum*." He said.

"Can I try it out, just to see how I do?" I asked.

"Sure," Walt said, "Come on down, I will set up a target behind the garage."

There is a rolling hill behind his garage that served as a backdrop to the target. How would I evaluate my performance with the *Bear*? Well, we found all the arrows. I had not shot a recurve bow since I was a kid, and I suddenly remembered why I got a compound bow. Still, I was undaunted as I continued to practice. I even managed to track down and purchase an inexpensive recurve bow of my own. I was shooting at a block target in the yard (outside of my beagle containment chain-link fence). The beagles were inside the fence, lounging in the shade and not paying much attention to me. Although I could swear that my Rebel dog gave me a look as if to say, "You can hardly kill a rabbit with a shotgun." I interpreted Rebel's look as constructive criticism and used it as motivation, as I gathered equipment, strings, arrows, shooting gloves, arm guards, and other expensive gear.

It was about this time that my stepson wanted to go see a superhero movie at the theater with some friends "Bob," he said, "Do you know where I can find any money?"

"You mean like in couch cushions and stuff?" I asked. What I was really thinking was "Good luck with that kid, I already raided the cushions for arrow money."

"No, I mean can you give me ten dollars" he said, looking at me as if I were not sane.

Luckily, for him, I was feeling generous because I had just done the laundry. When I say that I did the laundry, I mean that I searched all the pockets for money and returned the clothing to the hamper. His mother has a bad habit of leaving a fair amount of paper money in her pockets.

I have been taking block archery targets out with me as I condition dogs at the beagle club. I set up two of them 15 yards apart from each other. I shoot six arrows at each, and then move the targets 5 yards further apart to repeat. It is almost like pitching horseshoes against yourself--if the distance increased each round in horseshoes. And if you routinely lost horseshoes. As I nock one arrow after the other and send it at the target I am tempted to fetch my compound bow and make this whole thing easier on myself, but I keep shooting the recurve. Don't get me wrong, I won't take a bow afield every day for bunnies, but

I would like to shoot a few with a stick, just to say I did it. Mounting a shotgun is enough to make a stationary rabbit run away; I can imagine that drawing an arrow will be even more difficult. I have a little time until the season opens.

"I don't like that look in your eye," My wife said to me, just yesterday.

"Is it worry?" I swung and missed.

"No," She answered.

"Do I look tired? I feel tired. I have been in the woods very early a lot lately." I whiffed at another pitch.

"No, it isn't tired." She looked over her glasses in the fashion that a librarian might do, if she caught you with a cup of coffee and a snack in the library.

"Do I look thinner?" I asked, "I feel thinner, you know how I don't eat much in the summer?"

"Nope," She said you look like a little kid who just got away with something. I know you have some new hunting stuff, and I just can't figure out where you got the money. No big ATM withdrawals, No large checks."

"I don't know what you are talking about," and I walked towards the basement hamper—I am still losing way too many arrows. And if I ever get good with this bow I am going to want a costume, but not a kilt.

BUNNY GARDEN

Spring time is upon us! We may go straight to summer, given the mild winter, who knows. My childhood often found me paying for windows in the summer. There once was a time when kids had to be good athletes to make the sports teams. As a confirmed mediocre athlete, I never had to worry about the responsibilities of real athletes, like getting my sports equipment turned into the school or finding my varsity jacket to sew on a letter. It isn't that I was physically inept, mind you, it was just that I was plagued by a few athletic limitations. By a few limitations, I mean that I wore glasses, ran slow, couldn't hit a breaking ball, couldn't jump very high, and was relatively short until 11th grade. Other than that I was an animal.

Fear not, I was in good company. There were plenty of other kids in the same boat as me. We were the kids that played pickup games in large yards. Whilst the talented athletes were tearing up the athletic facilities of the sanctioned sports, the rest of us were playing sports amongst ourselves. It was actually a more dangerous game. There were no officials, and we resolved our own disagreements whenever a close play happened. Such conflicts did, on occasion, end with the exclamation of "I am taking my ball and going home!" or perhaps a bloody nose or black eye. More typically they were resolved more peacefully, but in such a way as to make the combatants, I mean participants, even more angry with each other. For instance, you, as the batter, might call a pitch outside (a ball) in the absence of an umpire. The pitcher clearly disagreed and would throw the next pitch at your hip. When the ball bounced of your thigh the pitcher would ask, "Was that too far inside?" You, the batter, then limped to first base. Also, we had no real equipment like the guys that made the real teams. Sure, we had bats and balls, but no protective gear like helmets or chest protectors.

Football season was when the lack of officials and safety equipment really got dangerous. Kickoffs looked like a war scene from a medieval battlefield, with kids being knocked senseless on both sides of the ball. All of our punts and kickoffs could have been filmed with slow motion cameras and the violence could have been set to Carl Orff's music for *O fortuna*. Naturally, even though we had pain, we had to walk normally around the house or our parents would see the degrees of our injuries and ban us from playing in any future games. Sometimes one of our players would make the real football team, and he would describe the experience under the coaches and referees as faster, stronger, but surprisingly a lot safer. "Hardly anyone bleeds like in the pickup games," my friend Bill said as a real jock. Summer was less violent, baseball tended to be not as physical, as most pitchers were reluctant to hit a batter with a fastball. There was no designated hitter in yard ball and everybody batted. A pitcher who tried to hit an opposing player could expect to be pelted with a high fastball himself as he stepped up to the plate.

Backyard baseball was more expensive than backyard football, as foul balls had an infinitely higher likelihood to shatter a window, rip through a screen house, or bowl over a row of clay flower pots lined up across a porch banister. A poor punt or pass thrown out of bounds in football seldom damaged anything. By the age of 12 or so we non-athletes were forbidden from yard ball, so spring and summer found us scrounging for activities. Fishing and spring turkey hunting were favorites for many. Myself, I preferred to follow my beagles as they chased rabbits. Of primary importance was the need to be out of our yards. Let me explain why—gardens.

One of the things that dominate downtown shopping districts now is farmer's markets. This is because the average homeowner today tends to only be able to grow lawns, and maybe a few flowers. This, of course, is no difficult task, considering the fact that grass will grow itself. At an alarming rate, I might add. There were no farmer's markets in my youth because no farmer thought he could actually sell cucumbers because every yard in the nation had cucumbers growing in them. People live detached from the land now, and they marvel at a yellow squash as if it required vast skill to grow. On Saturday mornings people go outside for the first time all week, having escaped from being confined to the indoors, and they go to farmer's markets. They go nuts over spinach," Oh my!" "Look, it is spinach, and cheaper than in the grocery stores!" "WOWEE! Green onions, can you believe it?" These people stare at the local farmer, as if he were an alchemist who had just performed some secret science to produce onions. Please understand that I am not implying that farming is easy. It is real tough, and I am glad that some farmers can sell their crops to the customer and make a little extra money. Farmers are the only people I know that sell all their produced goods for a wholesale cost and buy all of their needed materials at retail pricing. Ever looked at the cost of a tractor? I am just saying that many people don't realize how easy a vegetable garden is to grow.

After all, it wasn't too many years ago that vegetables were commonly procured from our yards. May was a good time for fathers to drag the tiller from the shed. My dad's tiller had giant tines in the place of front wheels, and it would bury itself if you were not careful. It had very little power directed at propulsion, and you had to push the behemoth forward. The longer it sat in one place, the deeper it dug. My father would cuss at his tiller for an hour or so as he tried to get it to start after having sat in the shed for the entire winter. He'd change the plugs, add some fresh fuel, a little squirt of starting fluid, a poetic discharge of profane words, the frantic pulling of the starter cord for a sufficient time to lengthen the right arm, and the machine was purring like a kitten. Next, dad would fight the monster to churn up fresh soil. The garden was made bigger each year, it seemed, which was fine because it meant less mowing. After the garden was tilled he would put a small fence around the tilled soil in order to keep rabbits out in the upcoming months. This was the end of dad's gardening. He was done in one day.

My sister and I got to plant seeds, weed the garden, water it with massive sprinkling cans when it didn't rain enough, cover portions of it when a frost threatened, and pick lots of vegetables. This is not to say that dad didn't help, but it was considered a chore suitable for kids. Especially if you had the nerve to sigh and say, "I'm bored." Such a sigh resulted in a hoe being placed in your hand and an order to go weed. Once the ground was tilled, a smart child got out of the house. You never knew when dad might send you out to plant onions, spinach, or some other hardy plant capable of withstanding the frosts of spring and early summer. I never slept late, and would gather my beagles at first light and head to the brush. Some mornings there was no need to go to the brush, because dad and I would go to the beagle club together—it all depended on what shift he was working that week.

Training dogs got me out of early morning weed pulling. This worked until I got home, and then there would be orders from mom. "You're dad went to work, he said for you to weed the garden when you got home." My only saving grace was that my sister liked to sleep in, and sometimes she had to weed or plant while I was in the woods. Oversleep got you more work than saying, "I'm bored." Dad was a firm believer that watering the garden in the early morning was better than doing the same in late evening, and I would often sneak downstairs in the morning to get the dogs only to encounter dad.

"Mornin' son," he would say, "Good to see another early riser. Why dontchya go out there with the watering can and give those tomato plants a good soaking before the sun gets up too hot. Then you can go to the woods. I gotta go to work"

Sometimes I would leave very early, keep the beagles out all day, tying them to a tree in the shade during the hottest hours while I sat by a stream to cool off before letting the hounds chase another bunny. I would return in the evening, after being gone all day, and dad would say, "Well, a good nighttime watering isn't as good as one in the morning, but why don't you go give it a whirl?" There was no winning. Which brings me to another point—no one wondered where we had gone. Kids today have their entire day structured by adults. They are in constant connection via cell phone, and it is a source of anxiety if a teenager's whereabouts is unknown for a few hours, especially at meal times. By contrast, I missed lunch all the time in the summer, and was informed by my sister that the response my mother often had was, "Good. I hope he is eating the food at one of his friends' houses, God knows I feed them often enough." And so it was. At noontime a horrified mom might see a boy strolling towards the house with a half dozen friends. Say goodbye to an entire loaf of bread, a jar of peanut butter, and a pint of strawberry preserves from last year's garden.

Rabbits, of course, are the perpetual bane of a garden, although a groundhog is probably worse. Yard rabbits can eat a lot of produce, but the more aggravating thing that they do is torment beagles. Duke and Princess, my first two beagles from childhood, were always quite vocal whenever a rabbit ventured into the yard. The fence that surrounded the garden, intended to stop such problems, never worked. I am convinced that this is why beagle clubs with poor habitat have no rabbits even with a fence.

You can put rabbits into the enclosure, but if the habitat isn't good they will find a way out. Duke and Princess had enough sight chases and found a sufficient number of dead rabbits during hunting season that they would go to full red alert whenever a bunny crossed into the property.

This, of course, was an immediate crisis. The noise might disturb a neighbor, or worse it might wake my father, who often worked nights and may not have gotten to sleep until well after sunrise. As a result, I tried to box trap the rabbits out of our property in the winter and take those lucky critters to the beagle club to be trained as professional athletes in the service of the beagles. To be honest, there weren't too many fast dogs to scare them in that club, as most of the members ran traditional brace hounds. My beagles were about the only hunting dogs in the club, and so only about one or two rabbits ever had to work hard when dad and I showed up. In return those rodents got mowed paths of clover and rabbit feed all winter.

Rabbits, as you know, breed like rabbits. So while the earliest part of the year may have found our yard bunny-free due to winter trapping, it would not be long before the neighborhood lawns would fill back up with cottontails. Sometimes, when it was too hot to run dogs, we would let the beagles have free reign of the yard. There was an outer fence along the property line to keep the hounds in our yard, and a smaller fence to keep the both bunnies and beagles out of the garden. The only thing worse than a rabbit eating your lettuce is a beagle nesting on it for a nap, ripping up the tender plants by the roots all the while. Duke and Princess would stalk the yard, and no rabbits would enter. Sometimes there would be excitement as the beagles noticed rabbits outside the perimeter fence, and the dogs would scamper under or over the barrier, with a dangerous chase through the streets ensuing. I could never box trap rabbits with much success in the summer.

We are decades removed from those childhood days. I now grow my own large garden. If my dad were alive he would probably like it, but he also would ask me why I have to plant it and weed it if I live with a teenager. I would have to explain that kids do not go outside. Adults don't either, and hence they think that onions are hard to grow and therefore they pay ten bucks for a handful of shallots. I place the garden outside my fence. The rabbits can get into the vegetables, but that is better than having them inside the fence that confines my house beagles to a small portion of the back yard. Let the bunnies eat some lettuce. All they have to do is have a few large litters of babies that all have a few more litters, and before you know it they will be forcing their own descendants to take up residency within the several running spots that I have within a half-mile of my home. I water the garden with a sprinkler at night—and the falling water keeps the bunnies at bay. But it does sometimes send the little critters inside my fence to eat clover instead. And then, when the beagles have their last bathroom break at night, I run the risk of a big chase through the streets of Ramey. Maybe dad was right, a morning watering of the crops is better after all. The bunnies can get more nocturnal feeding on my lettuce that way.

CARPOOL

Not too many months ago I was busted by my wife. I was being underhanded and deceitful. She caught me hauling dogs in her car. Few things bother her more than dog hair on the car's upholstery and the tell-tale smudges from wet noses all over the windows. I had tried to cover it up, but there was no way that I could keep it going. I began this indiscretion because gasoline prices were so high, and the car just got so much better fuel mileage than my truck. I was too lazy to put a plastic dog crate in the back seat, and this, no doubt, led to my capture. I found myself in marital court with the honorable Renee presiding, and I was found guilty and sentenced. I have since been paroled, and a striking development has occurred that has changed things.

At the beginning of rabbit season I was a in my first ever car wreck that was not caused by a deer. I am something of an expert on hitting deer, and I no longer even get nervous when I see the beasts crossing the road. One of the perils of evening meetings and Bible studies is the ever present possibility of crunching a deer on the way home. C'est la vie as our Quebec beaglers might say. But no, I was in a bona fide car wreck, and the important thing is that no one was hurt. I was the third vehicle in the billiards game, and my truck was heavily dented behind the driver's side door and my *Diamond Deluxe* dog box was sent tumbling down the road. Thankfully I was doing hospital visits and not hunting, and no dogs were inside. So all is well, right? Did I mention that this happened at the beginning of rabbit season? I had no truck, how was I going to hunt?

The insurance company for the driver responsible for the accident rented a car for me, and it was a very new *Chrysler*. My wife liked the car, and she allowed me to take her *Saturn* on hunting trips. It was a special dispensation from the marital court due to hardship. But I was hunting in a car! There is nothing convenient about meeting your hunting buddies in a little car. Instead of pulling into the parking lot with my truck and a dog box full of hounds, I arrived with a blanket on the backseat of the car to minimize the mud and shedding hair. Perhaps some of you have hounds that ride quietly in your vehicle as mine do. And, perhaps, your beagles also go to full alert as soon as you turn of the paved road and onto the dirt. They have learned that gravel roads lead to rabbits. I was meeting the guys at 8:00 a.m. to hunt. The fellows saw me coming up the little dirt lane driving my wife's little red *Saturn* car. The dirt lane was several miles long. This gave the beagles ample time to get their amperage raised. They were ricocheting off every window in the automobile by the time I got parked.

"You O.K?" Lenny asked as I stepped out of the car, my hat cocked sideways from a stray beagle bounce.

"Sure," I said, "Why?"

"You forgot to put a dog box in the back seat."

"I can only fit one crate," I said, "I could only put two dogs in one crate. I had four dogs to haul. They slept on the back seat until I left the asphalt—then they went nuts."

The beagle nose is legendary, and there really is not much distance between the back seat of the car and the trunk. I put my hunting vest and dead rabbits in the trunk for the commute home. The hounds could smell the rabbits in the trunk. They would shove their muzzles into the crack of the back seat cushion and snort, sucking the scent of cottontails into their nostrils. Then they would scratch as if they could tunnel into the trunk. They quickly threw the blanket onto the floor and commenced to plastering the upholstery with dog hair as they attempted to enter the trunk.

Traction is another worry when hunting in a car. I have taken four-wheel drive for granted. The little red *Saturn* was constantly at risk for getting stuck. Mud and snow are not the preferred terrain of this car. Did I mention that it has a little four cylinder engine that really lacks horsepower? The engine is so underpowered that you can measure the 0-60 time with a calendar instead of a second hand on a watch. When merging onto the interstate from the entrance ramp there is no way to get to the 65 mph speed limit before entering traffic. As a result I typically found myself running about 50 miles per hour while everyone else was cruising at 70. I can get to the speed limit within a mile or two. I can only imagine the thoughts of the truckers as they see the car laboring to reach the minimum speed with a pack of beagles in the back seat. That lack of horses under the hood makes mud problematic. I need to hit the mud puddles with high RPM, and enough forward speed to power though the soft spots. This means winding the engine in second gear as I tackle the mushy ruts. The car isn't real tall, and I often hit my head on the ceiling as I bounced through the water obstacles.

A dirty exterior, as you might suspect, is another problem. I can't return home with a little brown *Saturn*. After all, my wife knows that her car is red. So I need to stop at the car wash after the hunt and clean the automobile. The car wash change machine never works. No matter how recently the dollar bill may have left the mint, there is no way that the machine will accept it and give me four quarters. As a result I have had to raid my fun money. My fun money is a hidden jar where I put all my coins. When it is full I utilize the cash for hunting toys--collars, leashes, that sort of stuff (maybe some ammunition or a new gadget). At any rate the fund is depleted from the daily car wash visits.

The blast of water against the windows temporarily distracts the dogs from trying to shred the seat in order to gain access to the trunk. Although, I must admit, I failed to clean the undercarriage the first time I stopped to clean the evidence of the off road adventures. Imagine my wife's surprise when I left for work the next day, in her car, and the surge of power (well surge is an overstatement) from beginning to move forward dislodged hardened clumps of clay and mud.

There must have been a particularly large gob of mud under the front end that landed with a thud. I ran over this rock hard boulder of clay with the back left tire, and my head bounced up a little as the car climbed over the hardened deposit. I waved at my wife, who was standing by the window sipping tea as I drove away. When I looked in the rear view mirror, the space I just vacated looked as if a dump truck had unloaded its cargo. Renee was not smiling as I drove away. She frequently will mouth the words "I love you" as I drive past. I am not a lip reader, but I think she mouthed a bad word. Can you imagine if she would have seen how much of the mud I had washed off the night before?

It is also difficult to eat with a pack of beagles roaming the interior of your car. I often eat a snack on the way to the woods—an apple, or a few peanuts. In my truck I would let the food sit on the passenger seat as I drove. Well, no food can be left sitting with beagles on the loose. If I try to keep the food in my hand the dogs will try to get it. If I shove the food in my mouth, I am then assaulted with each dog's nose, as they take turns trying to smell my breath to see what I was eating. The morning coffee mug is also not taken along, because the beagles will lick the lid trying to get at the milk in the beverage. I tend to arrive at the hunting grounds under-caffeinated and hungry.

Of course the body shop was busy, and the repairs were not completed before deer season. So now I was deer hunting in this car too. I bought a box of those large lawn care garbage bags and lined the trunk. I then kept a tarp to roll up the dead deer before placing it into the trunk. I must have looked like a mob hit man as I was loading the blue tarp clad deer into the trunk. This was not exactly a scent I wanted to introduce to the dogs, and when I tried to load dogs to go to the beagle club I was paranoid about deer odor in the car. I did not want to create a deer problem and trash running where none had existed before.

Speaking of beagle club, have you ever tried to get in and out of a car without letting the dogs out? I had to slam the car door quickly before the mutts could escape. I then opened the beagle club gate, and snuck back into the car. I managed to get quite good at this, until, one day, one of the dogs accidently stepped on the power lock, locking me out of the car. The only good news about that little incident was that my cell phone was in my pocket and

I was able to call my wife and ask her to bring the other car key to unlock the vehicle.

Well, as you can imagine, I found myself in marital court again. I am forbidden to hunt or run dogs until my truck is repaired. I am told that the repairs will be completed by the end of the week. In the meantime, I am still eager to get out in the woods and run some dogs. I just don't know how I can get away with it. Anybody want to carpool? I would buy you gasoline, but I lost my change jar in marital court. I guess it is akin to the government seizing the property of criminals. Only it was my wife who seized my assets. I guess she saw me getting into that jar for carwash money.

CERTIFICATES AND ECOLLARS

People who do not run dogs in the wild fail to understand the value of negative reinforcement when training a hunting dog. In fact, I have found that in general we live in a culture that promotes only positive reinforcements and rewards. When I became a stepfather I was shocked to find that there are many events in elementary school where everyone gets a trophy. Sometimes they even buy trophies for the parents. Such a trophy might read, "Your kid got a trophy" When you read the kid's trophy it says, "Congratulations, you made the team." By the way, everybody makes the team now. I could letter in every sport if I went to high school today. Certificates of achievement are even more rampant. Our school district periodically complains about a lack of paper and the need to increase taxes. I have a stack of certificates thick enough to fill a four drawer filing cabinet. The certificates list achievements ranging from "Ties His Own Shoes" to "Demonstrates Vast Knowledge." If a child causes difficulties today the parents get to have a "one on one" with the teacher.

They did not have certificates like that when I was a youngster. They just gave you a bad grade and moved you into a class with kids that did as poorly as you. If your poor grades were the direct result of bad behavior (talking in class, bullying some kid and not paying attention) you, the student, might get to have a brief "one on one" in the hallway with the teacher. Teachers in those days owned paddles. Calling them paddles does them and injustice. Let's face it, they were works of art. My hunch is that woodshop teachers, at one time, were forced to demonstrate artisan skill in crafting a fine paddle. I say this because I had teachers that I knew were incompetent at building anything (although still great teachers) who owned exquisite paddles. One such teacher lived close to me and my father, after watching the guy paint his entire house, asked him "All those years in college to be a teacher and no one told you that most normal people paint a house from the top towards the bottom?" The house was covered in runs and drips as the guy painted everything he could reach from the ground before utilizing a ladder.

But these paddles were beautiful. When I say beautiful, I mean terrifying. Some were covered in tape, others had holes drilled through them to allow for a faster swing and a horrifying sound of whooshing air just before the moment of impact. Many were sealed with a clear coat or varnished to produce a nice, shiny effect. Some were elegant in simplicity, made of simple pine. Others were carved from cherry or black walnut. Many had rounded handles like a baseball bat. Male and female teachers utilized them, and each room had a peg, high on the wall, so that the weapon could be displayed. A few teachers even had their victims sign the paddle so that their younger siblings and cousins could read the name when they arrived at the same grade, and be scared into proper behavior. My name is on Mr. Woods' paddle. If any of the teachers who once paddled me are reading this, I have one thing to say: I will fight you now! I say this because at a rough calculation you must all be about 65+ years of age. This applies to all of my teachers, except my Algebra teacher, Mr. Tile. He has passed on to eternal reward, but when he was nearly 70 years of age he could still place his hands flat on a school desk and raise his entire body off the ground and hold it parallel to the floor for over a minute. He was one tough marine. I wouldn't fight him, even now. And he is dead (a great man, rest in peace), but the rest of you can come at me.

Ha! Just joking. I am glad for the few times I was paddled. Negative reinforcement does good things, at times. Current teachers everywhere reach their wits end and yell "YOU ARE ALL GOING TO GET A TIME OUT IF YOU DO NOT BEHAVE!" A few kids, no doubt, scamper in fear at this threat. Most keep running, jumping, screaming, and otherwise misbehaving. Gone are the days when a teacher grabbed the paddle from the hook and tapped it against his or her hand to silence a room. Occasionally, when an entire class was in revolt, a teacher would send 4 or 5 sacrificial victims to the hallway to expiate the sins of the entire community. Scapegoats would be lined up with hands against the wall and swatted in succession. Each child would then walk into the classroom with shame and fight back tears. Usually one kid allowed a trickler. A trickler is a tear that drips down the cheek with no other fanfare. Once in a great while we would get to see a full blown sob—the kind with very little noise, just a quivering bottom lip with the muffled sound of rapid breathing and a large snot bubble blown from one or both nostrils. One display of this sort corrected bad behavior in the entire class for at least two months. The pain, however, was minimal and brief.

What does all this have to do with beagles? Electric collars, that is what. Many dog lovers think that shock collars are cruel and unusual punishment. I think they save the lives of our beloved companions. If someone sees a *Tri-Tronics* sticker on my hunting vehicle they assume I am torturing the dogs. "Come to my house at night and see how abused they are," I always say.

"See what? How bad they have it?" they may respond.

"The fact that they own the furniture and eat the most expensive food in the house. I sit on the floor and eat bologna sandwiches."

I am not sure how it is in your state, but people can shoot dogs for chasing deer in Pennsylvania. Wouldn't it be crueler to let some overzealous deer hunter gut-shoot my dog than to correct the behavior with a collar? I know guys that really think a beagle is going to decimate the deer herd. A week long doe season with rifles (as we have here) might kill off the herd, but no rabbit hunter is going to have a beagle killing a deer. The woods do have guys looking for reasons to shoot dogs, or anything else, so training is essential.

My father hated deer chases. I once saw him catch two beagles that were pounding a deer and whoop them both at once. He was a whirlwind of legs and arms, and whenever one of the defendants seemed to be making a getaway they were drug back into the fray by a long arm. We walked the dogs out of the woods on leashes after that punishment and jumped a deer in the bed. Princess, the best beagle of my childhood, was led by dad over to the deer trail. She sniffed it and her tail wagged with excitement. Dad dragged her over two dead logs with haste. She never chased another deer.

I bought my first shock collar for a dog that would not down. I train all my dogs to down on command. By using down as a verb I mean that they drop on their bellies and cease moving until they are leashed or called to me. It is easier to catch the dogs and easier to protect them from dangerous hazards like roads and thin ice. My old Shadow downed fine in the house, and was almost impossible to catch in the woods. *Tri-Tronics* fixed that problem. I can down him at any distance he can hear me. I shocked him once at the age of one. He is almost eleven, and the last time we had an escape incident where the beagles went under the yard fence after a rabbit he obeyed perfectly. It has been nearly ten years since he received that one incident of correction from the collar. The collar is more humane than a switch or a smack. There is no chase to the dog or anger from running a mile to catch them. ZAP and it is done. I am not convinced the hounds even know the source of a shock. I have seen dogs get shocked on a deer and they run back to their owner in fear, thinking the deer scent caused the pain.

All of this being true, I must confess that I have not used a shock collar on my beagles in several years. I have a couple young pups, but all my other hounds are geriatrics and well behaved afield. As a pastor I have been in nursing homes in the evening when the nurses arrive with the nightly medications for the older members of my churches. They bring a pile of pills that nearly fills a *Dixie* cup. The cup's contents cover the spectrum of colors and rang in size from a sesame seed to a walnut (a walnut with the shell still attached, I might add). The residents of the home slug those down like a cowboy in a Western movie drinking a shot of whiskey—they make a grimace, but it goes down quick. The same thing happens at my house as we give each old dog a spoon-full of pills stuck inside a sphere of peanut butter. This has been the only way we can get the dogs to take pills, at least until they can make canine medicine taste like the feces of another dog. I really feel that would be a pill that all dogs would eat. In fact, you would have to hide the pills so the dogs would not overdose. But old dogs are obedient dogs.

I did, however, get to use the shock collar recently. My mother-in-law fell and broke her pelvis and now lives with us. No, I didn't put the collar on her. She has healed well and is quite mobile. She owns a yappy Pomeranian. My apologies if you like this breed, but I have not found anything useful in this particular dog, named Teddy (Teddy Bear is the pet name that her owner uses when she talks to him like a little baby). When my wife's mom moved in I had to alter the house. We converted the dining room into her bedroom so that she would not have to climb stairs. Both arched doorways into her room, which originally had no doors, had to be customized so as to accept a rectangular, insulated door. Insulation is necessary because apparently the television she brought to our house has no volume control, and it is stuck on the loudest possible volume. It so loud that my rabbit hunting damaged ears can detect it. She hoards the morning coffee into my hunting thermos and squirrels it away into her bedroom, or the "lair," as I call it (The Dragon's Lair) and we don't see her again until she gets hungry. She will then emerge and rummage through the refrigerator, looking remarkably like Yoda as he ransacked Luke Skywalker's gear in the movie *The Empire Strikes Back*. Otherwise you never notice she is in the house. But she has this dog...

Princess, named after my original childhood Princess, is a lemon and white beagle. She is a pretty little thing, all blonde and white. The Pomeranian, Teddy, has taken a liking to Princess. He is trying to claim her as his girlfriend. Keep in mind that Teddy is no physical specimen. If his hair was shaved I am not sure there would be enough dog left to see. The problem I have with Teddy is that he waits for Princess to go into the yard and pee. As a female dog she squats. Teddy then likes to hike his leg high and urinate on her back, claiming her in this way. I have never seen this behavior in any beagle. I got tired of bathing Princess every day before letting her back into the house. So I went into my office/den and brought out the collar that has not been used in years. I had to charge it, and then change batteries in the hand-held controller. The collar is old enough that you turn it on with the remote, there is no external button.

I must say, the collar looked big on Teddy. I thought beagles were small. It hung on him like a yoke. He wagged his tail and loved the attention. Next, I watched the 5 a.m. news so that he would forget the collar was around his neck. Finally, I let all the dogs out into the yard for the morning bathroom break. This is big fun for the beagles, which love to smell for any new critter odor from the night before. Sometimes a stray cat will be in the yard. Maybe some doves leave scent on the ground. All the dogs go through the search for the perfect place to relieve themselves. It must be difficult to require the perfect scent before going to the bathroom, but hey, I understand this to be the way things are. Teddy followed Princess while she looked for the necessary olfactory stimulation required for her to eliminate. She drifted from fencepost to fencepost, from the perimeter of the yard to the center, and finally, upon arriving under the ornamental apple tree, she found her spot. She squatted, Teddy raised a leg.

Teddy Bear stopped urinating in mid-stream and fell over on his side. I have never seen a shock collar deployed on the highest setting while on a dog with one hind leg raised. The dog did make a yipping noise. It was even higher pitched than his perpetual yapping bark. He stood up on all four paws looking at Princess. His nostrils flared to catch the scent. I lit him up again. He ran into the house. I never told my wife about the incident, but she knew something happened. The yappy little dog once loved to curl up next to Princess. She tolerated it, the way a popular girl in school will share one dance with the unpopular boy brave enough to ask her. Teddy won't go near her now. In fact, if she stands up to stretch, Teddy will run in the opposite direction. He thinks she shocked him, as if she were an electric fence that he urinated upon. I thought about hanging the remote for the shock collar upon the wall where Teddy could see it—you know, instill fear the way my teachers did with their paddles. But he has no idea it was me. It was a case, like Shadow, of using the collar one time only. I still haven't told my mother-in-law. I am using positive reinforcement to modify her behavior. I just gave her a certificate that reads "Shares Coffee with Others." She loves it. I hope she doesn't read the back, it says "Ties His Own Shoes."

GADGETS

Well, it was matter of time, I suppose, before I entered the 21st century with reckless abandon. I am talking about technology. I have owned *a tri-tronics* shock collar for years, but I haven't used it in nearly a decade. I bought it for Shadow, my nearly 12 year old beagle, who was almost impossible to catch in the woods. I trained him to "down" and he did it fine in the house and in the yard. He was not really a "downer" in the field, which was something of a downer for me. I must confess, I learned that negative reinforcement would work quite by accident. I was standing on a feed strip in the beagle club. It was deer season, and my deer tags were filled, so I was running Shadow dreaming about the second small game season soon to arrive, at the close of the rifle deer season. After a few hours of watching Shadow run some rabbits, I was ready to go home. I saw the rabbit cross a path, and I ran to that spot. When the dog appeared at the edge of the path I yelled, "DOWN!" By the time the final n was out of my mouth, Shadow was across the 10 foot wide path. This pattern repeated itself several times as the sun was setting. I would yell "DOWN!" and my head would be on a ratchet as I watched the hound flash by in the same amount of time that it took for me to yell the word.

It didn't matter if the rabbit didn't cross the path directly. On those instances where the rabbit emerged and travelled up or down the path before re-entering the brush, Shadow still bolted straight across, abandoning that rabbit in favor of finding a new one. He knew that if he slowed his pace to solve the check I would catch him, leash his collar, and we would go home. I typically caught the dog by diving, rolling, and otherwise performing maneuvers that looked like a cross between combat rolls and a very poor gymnastics performance. And on that winter day I made a snowball. I have heard that the Eskimo peoples have thousands of words for snow, describing different sorts of the wintry precipitation--powdery, hard pellets, big flakes, whatever. There is probably a single word for "the damn snow that I keep shoveling off the sidewalk and yet it drifts back by morning." The snowball I crafted that day was one of those snowballs that you make in the afternoon as the sun has melted a bit of the top layer of the snow. The water oozed a little as you squeezed and shaped the snow and you could really get a good, round projectile.

My glasses were in my pocket. They were covered in snow, water, and debris from the brush--all acquired and packed into the frame as a result of diving into the thick cover trying to get Shadow safely home for the night. In hunting season I often had to shoot a rabbit to end the chase, which is another story altogether. Suffice it to say that a dead rabbit was the sure way to catch him.

I held the snowball in my hand. I was angry—the dog handles perfectly in the house, the yard, or wherever. Hell, I take him into nursing homes to visit sick people and he is a gentle soul and perfectly obedient. He will even ignore the patients' food, a rare feat for beagles. Although, if you have ever eaten nursing home food, then perhaps you are aware of the need for many of the patients to be on dietary supplements! Not the tastiest stuff. Even so, most of the beagles I have owned would pounce on an elderly lap and use it as a springboard to get at the boiled, dry, chicken that seems to perpetually appear on cafeteria-served trays in hospitals and nursing homes. Shadow handles perfectly —in the absence of rabbit scent.

I saw the rabbit emerge from the thickets, run down the path towards me, and then re-enter the brush on the same side of the path from which it had appeared. I stood where the rabbit once ran. The big beagle chased the scent down the path along the line the rabbit left, until he saw me. He then ran across the path, and once inside the cover of some low-hanging hemlock he began to search for a new rabbit. I yelled "DOWN!" many times. He worked his way through the hemlock into a big opening. I yelled again, and hurled the snowball sidearm. Now, to say that I need my glasses is an understatement. I almost can't hear without them, let alone see. This is why I always get the frames that are nearly indestructible—the ones you can bend and twist and they go back to their original shape without any problem. I have no idea how I hit shadow with the snowball, especially with my snow packed spectacles in my pocket, but I did. It splatted, and a bit of snow clung to the side of a tri-color blur. He stopped. He waited for me to get there and leash him.

This was encouraging. I often worried about him being out all night with the coyotes, or dying from heat in the summer. I went home, and ordered a *tri-tronics* collar from *Lion Country Supply.* I shocked Shadow once with the collar. He has never refused to lay down on command since, not even on jailbreaks when he has escaped into the rabbit laden yards of Ramey, PA! He will down at 50 yards away.

And then I went back to a low-tech life, as far as beagling goes. I use bells to keep track of them in the woods. I have been hunting veteran hounds that are not deer runners, listen well, and are now getting too old to hunt much. Some time ago I purchased a *Garmin* tracking collar when the new model came out and the old one was cheaper. It then sat for over a year. My seasoned hounds went afield with nothing but a bell. There is something about the ringing bell that brings me comfort in the field. Then, I got puppies. Fast, enthusiastic, pounding, puppies, and I did not always know where they were. I decided to try the collar. I called Andy. He works at Lion Country Supply, and knows his technology (and beagles).

"Hello," he answered his cell phone.

"I need ya to help me figure out my tracking collar." I said.

"What's wrong with it?" he asked.

"Nothing, I don't think."

"You don't think?" he asked, "Call me when it is broken."

"I never used it," I said.

"You never used it? At all? Not once?" he was amazed.

"Right. Gimme a class. Wouldya?"

"Dude, you are gonna love it. Welcome to the 21st century, or are you even into the 20th yet?" He asked.

"I am in the early 20th. My Fox 16 gauge was made in 1929."

"Good Lord," Andy said, "I will meet ya tomorrow. What time are you done churning butter and making homemade soap?"

"I ain't that old fashioned!" I protested, "Wanna run at my beagle club before you go to work?"

"Sure, I will bring a pup or two." He responded.

It was quite a morning—both his pups tongued on a rabbit for the first time, and I learned to use the tracking collar. There is nothing like the tentative, but bold voice of a newbie learning the ropes as he yips, barks, and shrieks with a new world of rabbits opened wide. I hope I didn't make too much noise yipping and shrieking for Andy to hear his pups! The collar remote displayed distance, direction, and all sorts of data to tell you were your dogs are and what they doing. Technology is great, but I remember when this was not the case. As the pups started tonguing with some of my old hounds, I was whisked away into a fog of nostalgia, and I remembered a day when I had nothing but the lowest of equipment.

I rabbit hunted at 12 years of age with a bolt action 20 gauge. Dad thought it was safer than a pump action, double barrel, or autoloader. But, it had more ammo than a simple hinge action single shot. Not that you would ever have time to work the bolt to get a second shot at a rabbit. By the time I ejected the empty casing and jammed the bolt back into position the rabbit had entered the next county. Grouse hunting was even worse. The gun was not light, like my favorite guns today which sport two barrels and weigh less than 6 (or 5) pounds. No, this old bolt action shouldered and swung like a battleship turret. By the end of rabbit season my forearms looked like Popeye's from carrying the gun, which was a bit long for me, the stock apparently having been made from a load bearing rafter beam, with very little wood removed in the shaping process.

"It's too long," I protested.

"Good," Dad said, as I paid for the gun with paper route money, "You can grow into it."

I chuckled out loud at the memory as a tick crawled over my pants and jumped away from the modern sprays on my pants. I was wearing long underwear on that day afield, and I was not overheated. The new long underwear wicks the water away and keeps the ticks at bay. When I went afield hunting rabbits as a youngster, the only long underwear options were cotton. The cotton made you sweat. Of course the blue Jeans were also cotton, and the combination of cotton undergarments drenched in sweat and snow soaked cotton Jeans meant that you had to double the energy required to walk in them.

My boots then were waterproof. When they are solid rubber, you can keep water out. The felt lining and wool socks also kept water in, and the combination created a sweatbox. As a result, my feet were also drenched. So, after beating the brush and getting my body overheated, the dogs would jump a rabbit and I would wait for the shot. This worked fine, unless the rabbit was able to evade being shot for a prolonged time period. If the chase lasted for several circles, the hot feeling that characterized your legs and feet from walking changed to numbing cold as you waited for the rabbit.

This too hot/too cold shift was a bigger problem when deer hunting. After a mile or so walk into the brush I was sweating bad enough I had to unzip my coat. After an hour on the deer stand I was cold and had to walk around the tree to warm up. This packed down the snow around the trunk from the circles, and created an icy spot too slippery to stand upon. The solution to the slippery stand was to sit down so as to not fall down. Those cotton long johns drew the ice water right to your buttocks, which meant you had to stand again. I then moved to a downed log to sit upon and finished the day hunting from there, almost hoping that dad would return from his deer stand early and say we were done for the day. My lunch, of course, was comprised entirely of candy bars, that were jammed into the same green, bag-style fishing creel that had held dead worms not too many months previous. The candy bars were frozen. Biting through them required enough jaw strength that sometimes you broke through frozen caramel only to bite your tongue or the inside of your cheek, which caused a loud cussing to occur. I always wondered why I saw so few deer...

In the winter, the best part of hunting was to get to the truck, take off my boots and socks, and thrust them towards the blower vent under the dash. My hunting coat doubled as a coat for any and all non-school outdoor activity—heavy cotton that worked well until you got wet. A cheap orange vest was added, and it typically only survived one season. Of course there were a few years when some out-of-state hunters from Ohio were in our area, and they were not the safest of hunters. No doubt the sensible Buckeyes would not let these guys hunt in their Ohioan forests, forcing them to cross the border for venison. Pennsylvania welcomed them with open arms, and they were known to shoot at deer legs that were running through the pines. Dad made me wear orange snow mobile pants for those years, hoping to keep me more visible. They made my denim pants and long johns combination feel like *gore-tex* in comparison.

"I sure do love gore-tex" I said out loud.

"What are you talking about?" Andy looked at me with concern as I was transported back to the present.

"What?" I replied, watching the pups chase a rabbit past us and into the brush.

"I was asking you about installing the topographic maps on that tracking collar's hand-held remote. It is on a chip you can get. If you want to buy one, it will show you topography, roads, everything around." Andy explained

"Yeah, I want it," I said, "I like gadgets."

OLMSTEAD'S & THE HOG DAYS OF SUMMER

When it is too hot for the hounds to chase, an outdoorsman must have the wherewithal to find another pursuit. I try my best to avoid the television, because it is mind-numbing. One of the occupational hazards of being a pastor is the omnipresence of televisions in hospital waiting rooms. As if waiting for someone to come out of surgery is not stressful enough, people tend to watch useless talk shows in such circumstances. Frequently these shows revolve around the attempts of determining the paternity of a child born out of wedlock, the discernment of the sexual fidelity of a lover through a "lie detector" test, or some other sad commentary on society. The commercials are worse. I frequently put the television on PBS and watch Sesame Street—it raises the intellectual bar far above the shows geared for adults. All of this is to say that I do not find television to be a satisfying option for the rare evenings free from work. So, if the mercury has climbed beyond temperatures that I feel are safe to run hounds, I must find another outdoor activity.

One of my August endeavors is groundhog hunting. Large groundhog holes damage tractors and wagons. Shooting a few groundhogs, or woodchucks, does a great favor to the farmer and goes a long way towards securing permission to return in the fall to hunt bunnies. And sitting at the shady edge of a field is tolerable in the morning or evening. It is my "Thank You" to the farmers who permit me the privilege of hunting rabbits on their property. If you hurry and clean the fat rodents, and then cool the meat quickly, you can make the best pulled pork sandwich you ever had. Bring a sharp knife, as groundhogs are on the same level as squirrels when it comes to skinning them. Be sure to remove the nasty scent glands from the front armpits, throw the deboned meat in a crock pot, and wait for it to fall apart before adding your favorite barbeque sauce. I prefer the tangy (and less sweet) Carolina sauce. An old-timer who lived through the depression taught me the recipe, and it is better than it sounds. Hey, groundhogs and cattle have the same diet! Not long ago I was walking out of a farm field when the owner said "Got two more, huh? You're pretty good at hunting these things. Been at it long?" I stopped and felt waves of nostalgia washing over me, and memories of a hardware store...

...I was 13 years old when a summer trip to *Olmstead's* Hardware changed my life. It was an old fashioned hardware store that carried the basics of construction and home repair. *Olmstead's* was located in an older building, and the hardwood floors creaked underfoot. The store also catered to hunters by stocking ammunition, hats, gloves, vests, coats, and boots. I went in to buy my hunting license, and I noticed the deerskin gloves. Naturally, I had to have a pair. I quickly calculated the cost, and realized I had more than enough money to get the hunting license, gloves, and a box of .22 shells. My mother was in the store with me, as a minor could not buy ammunition. I begged her to take me because the Pennsylvania hunting license expires at the end of June, right in the midst of groundhog hunting (my new found outdoor activity when the heat was too much for the beagles).

I answered the questions for Mr. Olmstead who filled out the paperwork required to buy a new license--height, weight, eye color, that sort of thing. The license and gloves went into the paper sack with the shells. Mom was annoyed that I made her go to town, but I could not buy the bullets alone, and Dad was working. I hurried to the car, anxious to try on the soft, leather gloves. It was summer, after all, and I did not want to look too excited about the gloves in the presence of the store owner.

"Wait," I said, pulling of the soft gloves as mom started the car.

"Ugh," she sighed, "Now what?"

"I have too much money," I answered.

"Well, good for you!" She put the car in gear, shaking her head at my comment.

"No," I replied, "I had a twenty dollar bill and I still have more than ten dollars. They forgot to charge me for something." She put the car back into park and I ran into the store. Along the way I determined that Mr. Olmstead must have forgotten to charge me for the hunting license after he filled out all the paperwork. This was in the days before a license could be purchased with the swipe of a driver's license. It was before you could make an online purchase. This was when the store owners kept thick books that retained the pertinent personal data that accompanied each numbered hunting license.

"You forgot to charge me for my license," I said while walking in the door.

Mr. Olmstead was tidying one of the shelves where various plumbing elbows were stored. "Hey, you're right!" The tall man said. Then, and now, there is little profit in selling hunting or fishing licenses in Pennsylvania. Most of the fee goes to the state. I think the hunting license may have been $10 then. Probably $9.50 of that ten went to the state. The hope, for store owners, was that the person buying the license bought some other items—items with a higher profit margin. He would have lost almost ten bucks had I not went back.

I stood at the counter and paid for my license before running out the door, eager to try the gloves with thoughts of winter. Not long after that my dad was fixing something in our house and my mother was not home to go to the store and fetch parts. My mother routinely did this task for dad and he would measure, cut and prepare other items while the necessary parts were retrieved. This was before cell phones, so mom would always call home from the hardware store for a clarifying question about outside diameters on pipes, choices on various wood glues, colors for the chalk line, or some other detail that dad presumed the whole world knew as well as he did.

"Where is your mom?" Dad asked.

"Gram's house," I said. This meant my mom's mother. Dad's mother had passed away years previous.

"Oh shoot," he said, only he didn't say shoot, "Wanna ride your bicycle downtown and get some things for me?"

"Sure!" I beamed as he handed me a bolt with a washer and a nut.

"Get me ten of each item here. Just like them, same size and same threads. Tell him you want the same thread twist." He gave me some money and off I went. I peddled hard and fast and walked into *Olmstead's* store out of breathe with sweat trickling down my cheek. That is how kids travelled then, fast and with a sense of urgency. We propelled our bicycles as fast as they would go so as to get all the fun we could out of the day. Mr. Olmstead saw me in this condition on many instances, especially when dad was being paid to work at other peoples' houses and he needed a small item that could be carried in a small bag on a bicycle handlebar. I was a rural bicycle messenger. Dad said I was faster than mom anyway, because I never stopped at any other stores. She could take an hour in a grocery store, just getting a few items—she scoured the place for bargains.

I gave the bolt/washer/nut combo to Olmstead and told him Dad wanted ten just like it, "Same twist too, whatever that means," I said while daydreaming over the shelves of hunting equipment. He nodded his head in comprehension as he bagged the items. I paid with the money in my front left pocket, the money dad gave me.

"Anything else?" he asked.

"Well, I do need .22 shells for groundhogs, but I will come back when my dad is with me."

"I think I can trust an honest boy like you," he said as he winked one eye, "Don't tell the other boys."

I took my wallet out of my other front pocket and quickly bought the shells. I felt so trustworthy. I peddled home as fast as I could and gave dad his parts and change. I told him about the shells. "Good for you," he said, "Don't abuse his trust by buying ammo for your friends." I never did either. I would walk into the hardware store and slap my money on the counter, like a paying cowboy in from the trail and thirsty for whiskey, and Olmstead's would give me .22 shells. Always they commented about what a nice and honest boy I was. They just weren't around to see my sins, I guess (especially the ones as I got older!).

Several years later, at the age of 16, I was able to legally hunt alone. My friend Joe got a job bagging groceries for minimum wage, which was $3.35/hour at the time. I had some money from a paper route, but I was about to stumble on to bigger paydays. My father had found me a job shooting groundhogs for a few local farmers he knew. He conned them into paying me $2/hog after a few bad incidents of tractors running over groundhog holes and sustaining damage to the suspension. I believe there may have been a broken wagon axle due to a particularly large hole.

"Yeah," a farmer said to my dad, "I'll pay him two bucks per whistle pig. Won't cost that much. How many could he shoot?"

Well, the answer is that I could shoot a lot of them! Dad got several farmers to agree to the price and I was on the prowl with my .22. The profit margin really jumped when I was trout fishing on the river one time, just below a section that was designated as being for fly fishing only. I was using live minnows, trying to entice the few gigantic brown trout that I was wishing had drifted below the fly fishing area. Most, if not all, of the trout were above me— and not leaving the deep pools for the lesser section downstream. The trout weren't the only thing upstream, so was a guy clad in hip boots and a fancy vest and carrying an expensive fly rod. I, of course, waded with my old sneakers that had become worn, my toes peeking out the front. That is the the way that all of the other kids typically fished, we never had waders. The guy with the fancy gear was hauling one trout after another from the river, and throwing them back.

"What are you using?" I asked him.

"A fly that I invented myself," he beamed.

"Does it have a name?"

"Not really," he said.

"Do you sell them?" I asked, casting another live minnow into the shallow rapids below the good water as he hauled in another lunker.

"Nah," I only get to make a few each year. The secret is that I use a few of the longer hairs from a groundhog tail to make the fly. I don't want to run out of flies. I mean, it isn't as if I have an unlimited number of groundhog tails."

"Mister," I said, "Just what would you pay for a groundhog tail?"

To make a long story longer, I talked my way into making three dollars/groundhog tail from a guy that was going to sell the flies for a lot more. I was already making two bucks per woodchuck head, so I was now at $5 for an entire hog. The dumb woodchucks soon were gone, and I did not have the range with my .22 to get the smarter groundhogs I was seeing. I was frustrated at the limitations of my firearm.

Enter my half-nephew into the story. He was in college and about to be commissioned in the Army. He owned a model 70 Winchester .22-250 with 24x optics. He loaned me the gun for the summer. *Olmstead's* began stocking the ammunition for me. "Anything for you," Mr. Olmstead said.

My nephew, Kim, taught me to set up a rest on top of the mowed fields with hay bales, and how to glass for groundhogs. Then he was back to college. Actually, I think he left for Airborne School at Ft. Benning GA. I began my job as a professional groundhog hunter. I would be at the fields in those hot, humid days before the sun rose. You know those muggy August dawns when the temperature is already in the 70's before daylight? On some mornings we benefited from a rare morning of low humidity and clear skies on the previous night; and if this happened I would take the beagles out for a quick chase on the morning dew. I would hunt hogs at dusk on those days. Five dollars/hog meant I hunted every day!

It wasn't long until all my leashes were leather. I bought them from *Blett*, a guy that once sold leather leashes and collars from his business in Sunbury, Pennsylvania. He advertised in *Hounds & Hunting*. I also purchased some spill proof water bowls for the kennel and a screen that filled the back window of the truck cap. The screen provided shade when looking in the rear view mirror whilst the sun was blazing behind. No image was visible on the screen when looking out the cap, but people looking from the rear would see a beagle chasing a rabbit in full color. I really liked it, and so did dad, though he always claimed to like any Father's Day gift I gave him.

My friend Joe and I gathered one Sunday as the summer dwindled and school was about to begin. "How was work today?" I asked Joe.

"Terrible," he said, "I stocked the shelves and stickered the cans at the price they should display. Then they came back and made me re-tag every can after I was done. Somebody made a mistake."

"Bummer," I said.

"Then I was bagging groceries and all the old ladies wanted to squeeze my cheek when I took their bags to the car. They all know my mom and dad," he said, rubbing his cheek to remember the pain. "How was your day?" He asked.

"Rough," I said with a weary voice, "I am now killing woodchucks so far away that I have a hard time locating them when they die in the tall grass after I shoot."

"Are you serious?" Joe said, "That is your problem? Hunting is your problem?!"

"Yeah man. I sit at one end of the field and then shoot the hogs at the other. I have sticks to lay down pointing in the direction that I shot. I write down the estimated distance so I can walk out there and find them when I am done shooting, around midmorning. Some mornings I end up working until 11:00, by the time I find them all. I try to sit in the shade, but it still gets warm out there."

"Do you know how hot it is in the store room of the grocery store?"

"Nah, I hate grocery stores. I like *Olmstead's*."

LONG WEEKEND

Father's Day is a weakling in comparison to Mom's big day. This is in part due to the fact that fathers are not overly cognizant of the fact that there is a day in the calendar whereupon their children are supposed to dedicate a portion of said day to the 'ol progenitor. I am a step-father, and I am hoping my kid will emerge from his bedroom for part of the day. Maybe he will even go outside if there are sufficient enticements—food cooking. Otherwise, it seems more and more difficult to get children to go outside, even to play. I think there is a chance my son will come outside—if the food is out there and there are no tasty meal alternatives inside the house. It wasn't always that way with kids. I recall living the entire day outside in the summer.

To begin with we had to do morning chores. The yard and the garden were big ones for me. Once the daily chores were accomplished, the smart choice was to get the hell out of there before a mother or father found more work. I still remember many an afternoon where I made the mistake of saying, "I'm bored."

If my stepson says, "I'm bored," the entire home goes to red alert. The fear, of course, is that bored children will get into trouble. Drugs, alcohol, and enlistment in a gang are all worries, I guess.

"Should we play a game?" my wife may ask.

"Do you want to go to a movie?" my mother-in-law might chime.

"No..." the child's eyes might roll back in his head, indicating the severity of his boredom. His mother and grandmother panic, since they envision such extreme boredom as leading to bad life choices.

Finally, one of them will ask the magic question, "Wanna go get a toy?" The boy brightens, his shoulders cease to sag, and off they go to get some electronic doohickey that will send him towards a screen, monitor, or television.

No, I told my father I was bored on a rainy afternoon, just minutes after he returned from work, and he handed me paint scrapers. "Good" he said, "The porch needs painted. You are too sloppy to paint the porch, but you have enough talent to scrape the old paint away."

Notice how there was no concern for my long term self-esteem when he told me I was sloppy? That would probably be a cause to call children and youth today. Back then it was just the hard facts of life. I scraped the porch all afternoon until it was finished, or so I thought. Dad told me it was not scraped smooth enough, and I spent the next morning finishing the job so that he could paint it when he got home from work. As kids we learned to love boredom. Boredom was synonymous with freedom from menial chores.

It was rare for my father to be off work on Father's Day. His shift at the factory changed every week and his scheduled days off rotated through the week as well. These scheduled days off were rarely Saturday or Sunday. No doubt the actual rotation schedule was created by former Nazi war criminals that escaped Europe in the 1940's and became industrialists at the factory where father worked. The schedule was designed to get the most work from the least amount of hired employees, with the lowest pay they could negotiate. There was, however, this rare calendar oddity that seemed more elusive than an albino whitetail buck—the long weekend. My memory is fuzzy on this, but I think the long weekend happened when an employee ended one work week with two days off, and started the next week with two days off. Well, not really, because the long weekend always ended with Dad finishing that last day of the weekend by going into work at 11 p.m. Nevertheless, on occasion he would be home Friday-Monday. This happened on one Father's Day weekend.

Four days off seemed too long for father, and he often would take a job remodeling a bathroom or some such task that would supplement the annual income. Typically such extra income was utilized for stuff like groceries and utilities. Sometimes he would actually take the days off and relax—you know, by getting firewood for the winter, doing repairs around the house, or working in the garden. At other times someone would be on vacation during the long weekend and he would work overtime at the factory and never even utilize the scheduled days off from his job. I was hoping that the long weekend for Father's Day would be one filled with fun.

I remember talking to Dad on Thursday before Father's Day, unaware that the long weekend was happening. "Whatchya wanna do for Father's Day, go camping?" I asked him. I was a teenager, and I knew what buttons to push to get a reaction from dad.

His answer was predictable. "I camped for a year in the Philippine Islands during World War Two, I have no desire to camp again," he replied.

"I know. What are you gonna do for the big day," I asked

"I thought we would work—it is my long weekend."

"Work on what?"

He puffed his pipe and said, "On a kitchen. I can do it in four days if you help."

Great, I thought, a four day chore of fetching boards, sweeping sawdust, and measuring scrap ends for a piece of lumber that can be used to fit a particular place with the least amount of waste.

"You still want a litter of puppies from Princess?" he asked. Princess was our brag hound.

"Yes!" I stood up excited.

"Well, get the tools ready for tomorrow. When we are done I will be able to afford a new kennel, complete with a whelping area. I gotta go to work yet today, but we will start tomorrow morning at eight. We can't start any earlier because the house we are working in has retired people who don't want to get up any sooner."

I had a good idea what tools we would need, and began to get them all gathered so that we could leave in the morning. I brought the tools up the basement stairs, from his workshop, and stowed them in the laundry room, which was adjacent the driveway. From there we could quickly load the tools in the pickup in the morning.

Now, to call our laundry room a "room" is really stretching the definition of room. It was more like a hallway that did not connect any rooms. It was a tiny area as you entered the house from the side yard. Putting tools there was a tricky proposition, because it meant intruding upon mom's space. You see, the laundry room had barely enough wall space for a freezer, a hot water tank, a washing machine, and a dryer. I decided to encroach upon the dryer, which was seldom utilized, other than winter. My mother was a definite believer in hanging clothes on the line. Even so, I remember her dismay at finding the cache of tools in the room/hallway.

"Are you out of your mind!?" She yelled

"What's the matter?" I said, running to her voice.

"I can't get through here, these tools are stacked everywhere!"

Her term "everywhere" would be an exaggeration. In truth, it merely filled the entire space between the top surface of the dryer and the ceiling. Well, and the floor immediately in front of the dryer. The floor along both sides of the dryer also contained a few power tools. O.K., there were a few tools on the washing machine too, but they could be easily moved in a few minutes if a load of laundry needed to be done.

"Mom," I began to explain in a soothing fashion, "It is quite easy to get through. Here watch."

I placed one hand on the washer and the other on the exposed edge of the dryer on the opposite wall. These two appliances were situated opposite each other, with a narrow bit of floor (now covered with tools, neatly stacked, mind you) separating them. With a palm placed on each I lifted my legs and swung over the puddle of tools between them, landing gingerly on the other side.

"See," I said, "Just make sure you lift your knees to your chest so that you have enough clearance to get over the portable workbench. I have the legs on the bench set at the lowest height."

My first indication at her displeasure was the fact that her mouth was moving but no noise was coming out. As near as I can tell this phenomenon, common in mother, was caused by the words loading in her throat so as to gain power, the way you might store energy in a catapult for the ensuing rush of kinetic energy. When the words did emerge they were in fierce competition to see which would come out first. It must have been a tie, because the resulting sound was never a word, more of a guttural shriek. After the initial auditory blast she began to form sentences.

"Get that stuff back in the basement. Right now!"

"It took me an hour to gather it all," I whined, "We are starting at eight tomorrow morning, which means we are probably leaving at seven."

"Then I guess you better be awake by six to haul those tools back upstairs! Or you can put them in your father's truck when he gets home from work tonight."

When dad returned from work I was in bed, but I heard mom greet him with the words, "Guess what your son did?"

This was a typical question that my parents asked each other, "Guess what your son did?" It seems I spent much of my childhood with my parents trying to give me, and my culpability, away to one another. Although, to be fair, they both tried to claim me on the instances when I actually did something that might be deemed valuable or noteworthy in a good way. Before dad could guess she answered her own question, "He stacked all those tools in the laundry room."

"He's excited," is all he said. And I was. I wanted puppies. I was awake by five. I loaded the truck and was eating a bowl of cereal by six. We left early and unloaded the tools in the yard of the client before going to the lumber yard for the first round of supplies. When the family was ready to let us work at eight we were ready to begin. The job was basically replacing a sagging floor, building new counters, installing new cabinets, and plumbing and wiring a dishwasher. Dad did not build the cabinets. They were purchased by the homeowners. He did build nice cabinets, but they were a little more expensive than the family could afford. We finished Monday night at 10 p.m. I thought the retired couple would be a little upset that we were working so late on the last day, but they seemed to be pleased. It was not until after I became a pastor that I realized some retired people keep the hours of teenagers, sleeping late in the morning and hooting with the owls at night. This couple was of that retirement philosophy, I suspect. I am sure you know a few retirees of this persuasion. They are the guys who run dogs at noon at your beagle club!

At any rate mom arrived in her car at ten o'clock, as I swept the last sawdust. Father took her Buick directly to the factory in order to work until 7a.m. I loaded the tools in the pickup and mom drove the truck home. She hated that old F-150. The carburetor was notoriously finicky, and had to warm up, even in summer. Later that summer we built the kennel—it had four large, above ground wire runs facing south, and an above ground whelping kennel facing east. The whelping kennel could be utilized as a fifth kennel as well. All the runs emerged from a shed that was more aptly titled small building. It was insulated and had electricity. Some paneling and storage cabinets were inside as well. A cement pad was poured under all the runs for easy cleanup. We bred our Princess the following year, and pups were born in the spring. I missed the big event of the pups' arrival, as I was a sophomore taking the SATs for the first time. I was reluctant to take the tests, because I wanted to do carpenter work full time.

"Listen," Dad said, "Your carpentry skills really peaked at sweeping the sawdust." He was being serious, not mean.

"I can do a little more than that," I said.

"Well, true, but none of it comes easy to you," he said. And he was right. I can still remember helping him on certain jobs. I can picture him making his hands do the things I understood in my head, but was unable to make my hands do. My carpenter work is solid, sound, and ugly.

"What should I do?" I asked.

"Find something you are good at. And make enough money that you don't have to work on your long weekends," he said. I can only imagine if he had lived to see me finish graduate school. Not only are pastors not wealthy, we work every single weekend! He would have had to ask my mother, "Guess what your son did?" Happy Father's Day.

NOVEMBER FIRES

November is my favorite month, just as August is my least favorite. I would gladly trade August for a second November. November also marks the beginning of normal household heating, if you heat your house with firewood. As a kid we heated our house exclusively with firewood. This is much easier to do when you have a gullible boy in your house.

"Wanna do a man's work?" my dad asked.

"Of course," my ten year old vocal chords shrieked, my voice having not changed in the remotest.

"Go stack that firewood then." My father would continue. Ready to be a man, I would dutifully go stack the wood. Kids are no longer gullible. I asked my step-son if he was willing to do a man's work and his response was "Nah." He walked away with earphones on and video game in hand.

I was splitting firewood by 11. Granted, it was only ash trees with easy grain, but it was a task that was reserved for me, and all summer long I had a weekly quota to meet. Failure to meet that quota would mean restrictions in playing baseball, fishing, or whatever else we kids decided to do. If someone saw an 11 year old swinging an axe today there would be trouble—some state agency would pay the house a visit with concern for the child's safety. I could only imagine if such an official would corner my father about this sort of child labor when I was a kid.

"Mr. Ford, do you realize your son is out there whacking logs apart with an axe?" the guy would ask.

"Yeah," dad would have said with shame, "He is a bit puny for his age. I guess he does whack more than split. I am hoping he grows soon and can split 'em with one swing."

"What!" the outraged civil servant would sputter, "What if he cuts himself with that thing?!"

"He damn well better not," dad would have said puffing on his pipe, "I told him to keep his feet spread apart and to swing straight down. He knows if he cuts himself he will get punished."

It is good for my dad that he is not alive to parent or grandparent today, he would never make it. He would not understand the overarching concern that the current culture has for children's self-esteem.

The worst part about heating a house with firewood is the beginning part of fall, when the mornings were cold and the afternoons were hot. It would not be uncommon to see a home heated by a wood burning stove with all of its windows open, trying to get the house cooled off enough to eat supper inside. It might be 50 degrees outside and 80 inside.

One of my daily jobs as a teenager was to start a fire in the morning and get a bed of coals that would generate heat all day without my mother having to go to the basement to fool around with it. In the early fall I just started a fire before school and let it go out. Mom would be cooking later and that would be enough warm the house for the rest of the day. By November there would be a need to keep some amount of fire burning all day. This really cramped my style after I was old enough to hunt by myself, as I could not leave with the beagles on weekday afternoons or Saturday mornings until I had the fire burning well enough to last until I was done hunting for the day. Sometimes I would come home for lunch on Saturdays to poke around the firebox and stoke it before going out to pursue cottontails until dark.

Burning firewood is not as difficult as it once was. I now see mechanical, gasoline powered wood splitters in people's yards that prevent them from having to swing a variety of sledges with splitting wedges, axes, and other heavy instruments with handles. Wood is now typically spilt by feeble people who control the lever on a power splitter as somebody else feeds the logs into the contraption. It was all done by hand when I was a kid. I once counted how many times one must handle a piece of wood before it is burned. You (1) cut it down in the woods (2) cut it into lengths that are as long as the truck bed (3) load it into the truck bed (4) unload it into the yard (5) cut the logs into the length of the firebox of the furnace (6) Split the wood (7) stack the wood in the yard (8) wheel it to the chute that leads to the basement when there is room down there (9) stack the wood along the basement wall, and (10) burn it. It seems to me that I ate 10,000 calories per day and never gained weight as a youngster. Dad said feeding a hard working boy was cheaper than heating with natural gas, so I just kept on cutting wood until I left for college. That is when he bought the high efficiency gas furnace. When I got to college I was rather powerful, physically, for a college kid. Well, except for the athletes. It turns out I was lifting weights my whole life and didn't know it.

I often allowed the beagles in the basement with me while I built the morning fire. I should clarify what I mean by basement—it was a one room with cement walls and a cement floor. A sump pump was located at the lowest point for the spring months, when melting snow and heavy rains poured into the cellar. There was no finished ceiling either. You looked up at the floor joists of the house. It in no way qualified as a den, study, office, or man cave. It was all dug out by hand, and I remember not being allowed to sleep in my bedroom because that end of the house was "jacked up" with some large screw jacks while we awaited the cement trucks that were pouring the last wall. It was cold down there on winter mornings. I would let my two beagles run around the basement while I built the morning fire

This was in part to keep them quiet. Otherwise they would see me sneaking into the basement and begin yipping and barking in the yard. Like I said, it was a cellar, not a family room, and the only access came from stairs that were in the yard until we built an enclosed back-porch-storage-facility for more firewood (Ha, that is an 11th time to handle the wood!). So, I would walk through the screened porch, which was covered in storm windows through the winter months, to get to the cellar. The dogs, of course, would see this morning movement and begin to get excited. Every morning I let them join me in the concrete bowels of the house so they would be quiet.

On school days I would return them to the kennel before I went to school, on weekends or hooky days I would then take them afield for bunnies.

My basement now has a wood pellet stove. There is almost no labor in burning wood pellets, which is why I can no longer eat 10,000 calories each day without a negative impact upon my physique. It is also the reason why I would no longer characterize myself as powerful. It seems like not too many years ago that I would carry 200 pounds of dog food at a time when a club was stocking food for a field trial—a 50 lb bag on each shoulder and one in each hand. I would never try that now. My dogs live in the basement all the time, and my wood pellet stove is the focal point of my study—a dry room that never leaks, furnished with book shelves, padded seats, and even windows. Even this computer is in that comfy room. The church owned home is comfy. I do still let the dogs sit with me as I start the blasted machine. It throws a nice glow, and burns all day without needing me to touch it. Well, it is November, and I just got the fireplace started. I think I will go hunting before I do my morning hospital runs. It is cold enough to leave these house beagles in my truck after the hunt. I will just put brush pants over the top of my slacks, and a cotton duck shirt over my clergy shirt. No one will even notice at the hospital—unless they are careful enough to notice that I am wearing leather boots. Welcome back November, I sure did miss you.

OUTDOORS

In September I got the opportunity to do something I have always wanted to do—visit Alaska. I went to attend The Outdoor Writers Association of America's annual conference, which meets in a different spot each year. This year it was in Chena Hot Springs, relatively close to the Arctic Circle. Resorts are prepared for crowds, after all crowds are the goal of such places. There were a few glitches with hosting America's Outdoor journalists. One was coffee—there was a momentary crisis on the morning of the first breakfast when the coffee urn went dry. Being a resourceful lot, we tilted the urn to the point of having it sideways in order to get the last drop of nourishing caffeine from the vessel. There was a bit of a delay on the part of the staff in refilling the urn, and a mini-riot almost ensued. This problem never occurred again, as the staff quickly adapted to the copious coffee intake of writers.

The second glitch was also due to the nature of writers —the bar closed early the first night. For some, this was a bit of handicap. Alas, the place was full of Hemingway-like figures savoring booze and beer. I must confess I did have an Alaskan made beer (Shhh..what happens in Alaska stays in Alaska). Again, the staff, no doubt still muttering behind the writers' backs about the coffee intake must have had disbelief about the night-time beverage consumption as well.

This, of course, is just a precursor to describing the last glitch, a glitch that was ongoing throughout the duration of the conference—lack of internet. Wi-fi was available, but everyone was getting online at once and the result was slow connectivity. Many of us had deadlines during the meeting, and while in the midst of the wild beauty that is Alaska there were people glued to monitors, computers, smart phones, dumb phones, and other digital gee-whiz type stuff getting articles written for our editors. This last glitch leads me to mention one of the highlights of the conference, which was a presentation by Richard Louv, the author of *Last Child in the Woods: Saving our Children from Nature-Deficit Disorder.* His keynote address resonated with my whole being. People are too distanced from nature, even if it doesn't seem like it for us beaglers, who are perpetually afield training our hounds for hunting and trials.

When I was a kid, most of my time afield was confined to fishing and the constructing of tree forts, at least until I got beagles. The tree forts were actually tree houses, but we called them forts. We found abandoned tree stands for deer hunting and converted them into massive platforms by adding whatever lumber we could pilfer from our families. I remember one particularly sad day when I took a full sheet of plywood from home, only to discover weeks later that, despite it having been sitting in the basement for a year, the wood was not unwanted. I was about to be punished until dad asked me where it was.

"The coal mines," I answered.

"WHAT? How did you get it out there?"

"I drug it." I confessed, "Over a few days time." The coal mines were not in use, and had been reclaimed by the surrounding woods. Blackberries and hemlock were starting to return. It was several miles from the house, and the place where I felt most at home. We had cut the sheet of plywood with an old rusty hand saw at the site, and made an extension on the tree fort--a higher level looking west. Somewhere, deep inside, I knew we must have been stealing the wood, or we would have cut it at home in order to make the transport of the wood easier. Instead we scampered into the tree line with this heavy board in tow like a house beagle who had just absconded with something from the kitchen table.

Tree forts were our summer homes. No one looked for us, and no one worried if we were out late. These arboreal abodes were stocked with comic books, hunting magazines, and BB guns. We were quite willing to live on berries all summer, supplementing that diet with whatever other food we could scavenge from home. I remember days of onion sandwiches, where we took a handful of garden onions and a loaf of bread with us as we ventured into the cover of our own forested playground.

Today, the presence of kids outside is not as commonplace. Kids walk in a daze with their eyes glued to the plethora of screens that accompany their every moment, ear buds stuffed into their ears to further isolate them very the very world around us. I teach a few college classes in philosophy, and cell phones hum throughout the classroom as students receive a blitzkrieg of text messages from their peers. While I am normally able to keep their attention throughout the class, they still have their phones on standby, collecting all the instant communications that they desperately need. When class ends they all walk away, staring at a phone. They don't seem to be outdoors for long.

Beagles force me outdoors, and I am glad for it. I still remember with fondness the day that I got my first beagle pup, and how he puked all over me on the way home and my mother had to run into a store and buy a tee shirt for me to wear for the remainder of the return drive. I pitied the poor carsick hound, and held him close despite his vomiting attack. I brought him home in June, and had the whole summer to spend all the daylight hours with that dog. Mostly we sat in the yard (the great outdoors to many kids nowadays) but I also took him to the beagle club with my father, who had bought a female half-sister to my pup on the same day. Duke and Princess were my constant companions that summer, and both were chasing rabbits by four months of age.

I was devastated when school started at the end of that summer. I had to leave my hounds for the annual revocation of parole and the subsequent return to the incarceration of school. How would my hounds get by in their kennel all day without me? The first thing I did when I got home from each school day was to let the dogs run around the yard, and maybe go rabbit hunting if I could find someone to take me—I was not yet sixteen, and so I could not hunt alone. My dad gladly took me when he was not working, but if he was at the factory I had to beg any number of adults to go afield with me. I anticipated the hunting season all year long.

I was the only kid in our beagle club, or the only one who actually went there with any regularity. I had the combination to the clubhouse, and was given permission to carry a .22 whenever my father and I ran dogs. The rifle was for the purpose of controlling feral cats that viewed our running grounds as a buffet table stocked with rabbit meat. Beagles were my passion, and I suppose it is no surprise that they still are. My current hounds live in the house, so I get to see them a lot. I almost forgot those feelings of woe I had as a kid when I could not see my dogs very much due to school. I forgot about running my dogs at the coal mines until they were too tired to chase anymore, and then sitting with the hounds under a shade tree before walking home. I forgot about sitting under the plum bushes in my yard, which had grown tree-sized, and patting the beagles on the head as we whittled away the hot hours of the summer, waiting for the sun to sink lower to the horizon, before going for a short rabbit chase before sunset. I had forgotten about early autumn, pre-hunting season chases, late in the evening when scenting conditions were strong. These chases were so good that I almost always stayed out until it was quite dark. And I had forgotten how a pair of tired beagles could guide a boy home on the most overcast night, navigating the darkness with their keen noses, so long as I kept them on the leash and prevented them from running another rabbit! I never carried a light, and my GPS was a pair of tri-color bunny-busting beagles. I had forgotten all these things, until I listened to Mr. Louv and his discussion of the fact that kids really do not get outdoors like they once did. Kids are not "in the woods" as many of the readers of Hounds & Hunting were in their childhoods. And then I started to think that outdoor writers better do some things. We need to do more than write. I think I want to buy a kid a beagle puppy, or give away a few of my fishing poles. God knows I have a shotgun or two that I don't use—some kid, and his father, should own these. I live in Pennsylvania and many traditional brace clubs have become gundog clubs simply because no young people were trialing brace hounds. The same thing could happen to gundoggers, as our sport isn't exactly full of kids. It is October as you read this, and small game season is in full swing. I serve as a beagle club secretary—not exciting stuff. I work on the field trial committee, and that isn't real fun either. Let's face it; a field trial isn't fun for a kid if their dog doesn't make second series. Hunting, however, is always fun. Maybe we beaglers can take a day this fall to be ambassadors for beagling by taking a youngster rabbit hunting. Rabbit hunting has lots of shooting, great hound music and allows the hunter to feel a heavy game vest. Otherwise, writers may have problems even bigger than coffee shortages, closed bars, and wi-fi outages. We may not have any sportsmen to read what we write.

OUT OF THE CLOSET

I will let you in on something that is no secret to anyone who has known me. I'm a nerd. There may be other terms that are used to describe people like me, but that was the common title when I was a kid. Remember the guy that carried a scientific calculator in school all day long because he had three science classes and calculus? That was me. I understand that this is now seen as a social asset, but I have a hard time believing such tales. When you show up late to lunch because you were really interested in a chemistry lab, you tend to get teased.

Still, I must provide the disclaimer that I was an Appalachian nerd. This meant that I spent all my extra time in the woods. I lived to chase rabbits, catch trout, and hunt deer. I was seen as an oddity in the nerd world when I moved to college because I fished, hunted, and ran after hounds. In high school, however, I was just a garden-variety bookworm. Every guy in town was an outdoorsman. In fact I remember high school biology class and the task of dissecting a cat. There were all sorts of detailed instructions on how to do this, which most people followed religiously. You would not believe how dull the blades were that we had been given to skin said cat. The tips were blunted from overuse, and the blades themselves were nicked and rounded. What were we to do?

Well, we whipped out our pocket knives. I had a very nice *Victorinox* Swiss army knife that I carried everywhere, and used most of the tools in one science class or another. My lab partner was George Machcoviak, and as my memory serves me he had a *Case* pocket knife that he carried for shop classes. This was in the olden days, when boys carried knives to school and no one got stabbed. This is also back when students got paddled, most kids could not make the sports team, and even more failed to get an athletic varsity letter, ribbon, or certificate on awards day.

Modern education feels that every child needs a daily trophy in order to boost their self-esteem, and sports rosters seem to carry a 5th string team for every sport.

I remember when boys got caught chewing snuff and were sent to the principal's office. The boy got paddled, and the principal kept the snuff. I just had a very polite and honest teenager donate 8 hours of community service to the church because he was caught in school with snuff. The school called the cops, and the kid was sent to the judge and sentenced 8 hours of community service. I know the judge. He chews snuff like my high school principal did.

In fact the judge is our head chef for chicken barbeque fundraisers at the church. The first time we held that BBQ I was chased like a common criminal. The problem was that I picked up three hundred halves of chicken from the local grocery store, and did not pay for it. To be fair, I was told to just take the chicken by the crew on the store loading dock. The store owners are parishioners of mine, and I was told that we were getting a very heavy discount, and to not sign for anything. I arrived at the fire pit a few minutes later with a store employee in my mirror.

"Where are you going?" She bellowed as I got out of the truck.

"Right here," I answered, thinking it was obvious.

"You stole that chicken!"

"Oh, no ma'am, I was told to wait until later for the church to pay the bill."

"Who said that?" She humped.

"The Moyers," I answered.

"And who are they?"

"The people who own the store where you work," I explained.

"Don't worry about it," The judge said, squatted and stirring the sauce over a low fire. The sauce was made with massive amounts of butter and vinegar, and the judge had a big dip of snuff under the bottom lip, "If it comes to my court I will throw it out!" he joked.

The store employee looked at the judge, clearly recognizing him, and then looked at me before asking, "Who are you?"

"The Moyer's pastor." She mumbled something about judges and pastors and we never saw her again. I wonder if the magistrate confiscated the can of chew from the kid before he sent the criminal from the courthouse with a sentence of eight hours.

Anyway, I digress. Once George and I produced our knives I looked at the directions.

"George, they want us to skin this thing like a fox hide going to market, but we aren't using it for anything that affects our grade, so why would we go to all that trouble to keep it in one piece."

"Fudge it," George said, "Let's skin it like a rabbit." Only George never said fudge. I mean maybe he did if there was fudge for lunch, but I never heard him. We slit the hide across the back and pulled half of it down over the hind legs, and the other half up over its head.

"Ford," George said, "Do we need the head for our grade?"

I scanned through the instruction book, and found that all of the assignments dealt with the gastrointestinal and muscular systems. "Nope," I answered as I heard the sound of George finishing the skinning. Our teacher was offering sage advice to each lab team. I could hear her talking about knife placement and safety. The rest of the class was just getting started with the hide removal. Our cat was ready for dissection when the teacher arrived. "Oh my," She said, "That's different than the instructions." She looked down at the lab table. There was our cat— skinless and headless.

"More than one way to skin a cat," I said, which I thought was witty.

"Where is the head?"

"Attached to the top of the hide over there," George said.

"Snapped right off," I said. George has some real strong hands. Plays lineman you know?

"Your knives are dull, so we are gonna use ours," George said.

"Yeah," I said, "Especially since it says that we gotta keep the gut pile intact to separate all the pieces."

George and I aced that lab. He could guide that pocket knife like a surgeon's blade. And that is what I mean by my being an Appalachian nerd. I was obsessed with the natural world, and I spent all my time studying. I would run my beagles and carry a field guide to trees while the beagles chased. Bird watching was another favorite study, and a properly maintained beagle club is filled with more varieties of songbirds than any other cover I have ever seen.

I belonged to an old brace club where I was one of the only gundog members, I was young, so I got to drag a plastic toboggan and fill the rabbit feeders with corn pellets in the winter. I remember looking at frozen ice crystals under a magnifying glass, trying to see the beautiful patterns in our science textbooks. I loved to find the maple trees at the club during early spring and eat the icicles from the limbs, as they had a sweet sugar taste from the running sap that mixed with the ice. I had gathered some rudimentary tools: a microscope, a rock hammer, a cheap telescope, and some books.

Now, I should explain that my sister had a large bedroom. My father believed that girls needed space, and boys did not. My bedroom gave me two choices as to how the room could be used when standing. I could face the dresser, or I could slowly turn and face the bed. That's it. The room was big enough for a bed and a dresser. There was a big storage room attached to my room, but it was full of things that spent most of their life in storage— decorations, keepsakes from my parents youth, photograph albums, winter boots that only appeared for winter, sandals that only appeared for summer, that sort of stuff. Where was I supposed to put my telescope and things?

We had a closet in the living room. When you opened the door you were looking at the underside of the steps leading to the second floor. The closet only extended a few feet before a person could not stand upright. Then you had to bend your knees before walking any further. In other words, it was almost as big as my bedroom! I placed books back under the steps, and stored my other things on the perimeter of the closet. I made a makeshift desk against the stairs at a point where I could sit, but not stand, due to the rising stairs. I covered the wall with geologic maps, a periodic table, constellation guides, and wildlife identification charts. I had my own study in there. At night there wasn't too much to do. We had CBS, NBC, PBS, and ABC. ABC didn't always have the best reception either. I would often go into my "study" and read or write. I would emerge when I got thirsty or had to go to the bathroom. The sudden opening of the door startled everyone in the living room.

Sometimes my mom would be on the couch and say, "Where's your brother?" to my sister.

I could hear her through the door and would emerge, "Right here, whatchya need?" This would startle mom and she would jump. "Get outta the darn closet!" she would yell. Only she never said darn. Yep, I guess you could say that I was a closet nerd. It was always a social liability being the studious type, and I tried to keep it quiet. No one needed to know just how many *Star Wars* toys I had. Hey, if I had more than one chess board there was no reason I had to advertise that fact. But, I am out of the closet now—I am a public nerd. No sense in trying to hide it. And I have an entire study. It comes complete with book shelves and a wood stove. I still love science, but theology and biblical studies comprise the bulk of the study/library, which is located in the basement. My computer is down there, and I do not hide from my nerdy nature. It actually has been an asset later in life. I suppose men like to have a den to retreat towards when domestic life becomes chaotic, but my room really is a study. I like to go there and let my mind roam. I'm still an Appalachian boy, so I plan hunts from that room. In fact it was at my computer by the fire where I wrote a column once that said I wanted to hunt swamp rabbits because I never saw one before. A reader wrote to the magazine where that column appeared, and the next thing I knew I was headed to Alabama. I teach college part-time, so I had to schedule the trip around Spring Break, but I was elated to see rabbits swimming like beavers. I brought some meat home and one swamp rabbit was left intact. No, I didn't dissect it! I took it to the taxidermist. As I delivered the rabbit to the taxidermist I also remembered a snowshoe hare that had been at a taxidermist in upstate New York for years.

The Swamp rabbit came back and still no word from the Empire State's taxidermist. So, on a trip home to see her family my wife stopped at the guy's house. She was real insistent. The guy took her to his studio which was so full of unfinished work that it took him a half-hour to find the varying hare amongst the filled freezers. I shipped it out to the same taxidermist that mounted the swamper. It just returned and looks great. These two bunnies are the only trophies I have on display. I have decided to look for more species of hare and rabbit that are absent from my home state (although we do have a few hare).

Actually, they freeze-dry small animals like rabbits now rather than try to skin them. They remove the entrails and fill the stomach cavity with crystals of some kind. They look very good when they return. A word of caution if you decide to do the same thing with some bunnies: a stuffed rabbit can cause havoc if you keep beagles in the house. I am not sure how much scent the trophies emit, but I have seen a sight chase or two break out as a snoozing hound looks up and sees a big 'ol swamp rabbit on the shelf.

The first time this happened I was fast asleep on the couch when my beagle Lady-Day went nuts in the middle of the night. At the time I only had the swamper back, and it sat on the television. I had fallen asleep watching the news and the light from the TV provided enough illumination for the rabbit-wise hound to see the silhouette of the massive bunny. The only problem was that I didn't know that was the cause of the ruckus. I was all over the house looking for the problem before I saw her jumping up in the air towards he television. I moved the swamper to my bedroom dresser with the same results. So now both mounted rabbit hunt souvenirs are located on the top shelf of my study. Sometimes they distract me as I dream of other hunts to pursue other rabbits with beagles. I want to hunt European hare. I would be thrilled to see a marsh rabbit.

If any of you young readers are nerds in school, cheer up. The day will come when you will be able to get a job you like and maybe make a hobby like beagling a passion for life. The teasing will end, and you will find there are plenty of people of the opposite sex who want to date nerds. I was told at my high school graduation that the best days of my life were gone, and it was all work from there. This proclamation came from a teacher! I will tell you a secret: that was a lie. Heaven help us if the best days of our lives involve raising our hands to go to the bathroom, although I do have fond memories of science classes.

SPRING CLEANING

I grew up in a house that took spring cleaning seriously. All cleaning, really, but the springtime scrubbing of every surface was a major priority. We heated our home with a wood stove, and while spring was a season when a few more fires would certainly be stoked on a few mornings to heat the floors in the wait for warm weather, it was certainly past the coldest party of the year. A warm March day would result in all the windows and doors being opened in the attempt to clear the house of all dust and debris that accumulates from a winter spent with wood. Wood chips, saw dust, and wood smoke stains were kept at bay while the snow was flying, but they always re-appeared. Come spring, they were all eradicated for summer.

The exterior of the windows was cleaned and every effort was made to clean the basement floor as if it were constructed of fancy ceramic tile rather than cement. If you have ever lived in a house that burns wood you know that even with the best filters in your heating system, the forced air heat will slowly add a thin layer of attached grime to everything over the course of a winter. If you have ever burned coal, then you know that the heater will transform your white walls into a color akin to tar. We burned wood.

Mom waited with glee for a warm spring day when her cleaning solution of bleach could be applied to the walls and allowed to air dry with the entire house opened to ventilate the fumes. The only odor that surpassed the intensity of spring cleaning was in the early fall when dad ground his homegrown horseradish into a paste of nasal clearing condiment that may qualify as weapons grade. It just might be a biological weapon if tested by the government. I know that any complaint of a stuffed nose preventing a child from labor during the flu season resulted in that child being served a sandwich with about two tablespoons of ground horseradish barely inside the top slice of bread. You were simply told, "Eat this." When the tears and convulsions began to subside you would then get a bath towel to wipe your nose. The bonus was that the heat from the horseradish disabled your taste buds for about a week, which made school lunches easier to take.

Dad would stand over the blender making his potent concoction with tears rolling down his face as the invisible horseradish vapors encircled him, "This is gonna be good," he would sob as he added white vinegar to the ground root. Chopping onions is mere child's play compared to horseradish production. I wouldn't drink a milkshake from that blender no matter how well you cleaned it.

One deplorable task was to spring clean the yard. This required a shovel and a garbage bag. Our dogs lived in a kennel behind our house, but had lots of time to roam around the fenced yard. Winter snows made it nearly impossible to find the canine poop that was deposited. Throughout most of the year I would walk the yard and gather it for the garbage man on weekly basis. To be fair, most of the beagle landmines were deposited in their kennel or in the woods. The kennel was cleaned daily all year long. The cleaning of the yard was largely ignored once the snows started. Spring thaw always revealed a landscape that at a far glance displayed nothing of any note. Close examination, however, would show a fecal death trap for any lawnmower that might be pushed through the yard. I escaped the bleach odor of the house by picking up the *Purina* remnants, which should be a good indicator of the intensity of the cleaning that was taking place in the house—I preferred doggie doo doo over the *Clorox*.

The beagles would bark incessantly whenever they saw me in the yard, so I typically let them out while I worked. This was true whether I was doing yard work, splitting firewood, or weeding the garden. The two beagles ran through the muddy yard (which had just lost its snow cover) while I continued to scour the yard. Did I mention that the doors to the house were opened for ventilation? I can still remember the screaming like it was yesterday. At first I thought mom might have fallen on a wet floor or cut herself with some tool. I ran into the house to see her swinging a broom at beagles, which were busy depositing muddy paw prints everywhere. She was angry when they scooted across the kitchen linoleum and slapped their wet bodies against the new dishwashing machine. She was in a rage when they proceeded onto the carpet and furniture in the adjoining living room.

After plowing their bodies into the furniture cushions, the hounds bounded into the front room where they decimated the pile of papers that sat on the coffee table. Those were the weeks' bills, school permission slips, birthday cards to be mailed, and any other documents deemed "important." After the whirlwind of dogs was finished the papers were mostly mud smears. I had not seen most of this devastation, because I was closing the front door so that the dogs could not get out onto the road. They had entered the house from the backyard, which was fenced and semi-secure (note: there is no secure fence with beagles in the event that a cottontail is within sight outside the fence), and I feared they might exit the house through the front door. A wild broom swing missed the pooches and smacked my backside as I was closing the front door. Mom was not concerned and kept swatting at the beasts. She would have been happy to send them out the front door, and there was little remorse for landing the broom's working end on my hind-end. In fact, I am not sure it was an accident.

The beagles were unaffected by the broom barrage, and proceeded up the stairs and into the bathroom which shined with the intensity that can only result when a stay at home mom puts her everything into scrubbing it. The two dogs had been fighting the entire time over a nasty old wet work glove that had wintered in the yard. The tug-of-war blasted out of the bathroom and into the hallway where I had a good idea come to mind. "Good" ideas were a rarity in my youth. My wife says they are nonexistent in my adult years. Anyway, my youthful good idea blossomed and I yelled "Down!" Both dogs dropped to their bellies. I picked one up and then the other and walked into the backyard with the duo.

"Why didn't you do that before?" Mom growled.

"I never thought of it." I answered honestly. Down was one of the first things we taught the dogs. When they were pups we would stomp behind them and it would scare them enough to drop to their bellies. We said "Down" while we did it. They learned it easily. It was how we caught the dogs on a chase in order to go home—if you were reasonably close to them when you yelled the command. It was also how we kept them off the roads during hunting season or away from "high walls" (they can look like cliffs) at a former strip mine if looked too steep to descend safely. Other than taking dogs off a chase to go home, it was pretty much a safety device only used in emergencies. The broom was starting to look like a viable threat that would meet the criteria of emergency when the idea came to me.

Beagles live in my house now, and spring cleaning has taken a new meaning. Sure, there is still the cleaning of the yard for *Purina* remnants, but the snows don't stay all season long anymore, and I can do this job throughout the winter during the periodic thaws. Gone are the days of my northwestern PA youth when wind off Lake Erie deposited a couple fresh inches of snow every night. My wife still gets the exterior windows in the spring as my mom did, and scrubs walls and floors. Dog hair is the work my mother would not have tolerated. Most books will tell you that beagles do not shed very much. This is a complete lie, and spring is a shedding season. Running the dogs in the woods helps tremendously as the briars will do much of the grooming for you, but the only way to keep up with the spring shedding is to brush them every day. The alternative is to have my wife come downstairs for work in the morning wearing black slacks that are covered in tri-color hair. When this happens she has urges to hit me with things that weigh considerably more than a broom.

I can tell when a beagle wardrobe malfunction has happened only in daylight. Sometimes the fine white hairs are mostly invisible until you walk outside into the sunlight which reveals everything. In the spring, my wife and I may be slightly late to work because of the shedding. We have one of those sticky-taped lint brushes and we can be found in the yard, both running late for work, grooming each other like chimpanzees to rid ourselves of the hair. I am an early riser, and will often throw my clothes into the dryer before I leave for work, and allow the tumble-dry permanent press to remove the hair. When I remove the lint from the dryer trap in the spring and lay it flat it resembles a small hide stretched in a trapper's shed, the ratio of dog hair to clothing lint being very high.

Spring is also the time to take care of my dog food weight circles for coupons and other prizes. Throughout the year I cut the circles and attach them to the basement freezer with little magnets. When spring cleaning comes and the basement gets scrubbed I will get my one warning. "If you plan on redeeming those circles, you better do it quick before I throw them all away. They look terrible on that freezer." The same conversation will occur in the fall. I can tell you that the time allotted between the warning and the disappearance of the point circles is less than one day. I know this because I once spent an evening with a head mounted light rummaging through the church dumpster looking for my weight circles. This, of course, caught the attention of the local cop who was patrolling the neighborhood. He was not impressed with my answer that I was looking for dog food bags, or portions of dog food bags.

Speaking of dog food bags, *Purina* no longer makes paper bags that can be ripped with reasonably strong hands. Instead they have plastic, fibrous bags that require my sharpest hunting knife to remove the points circle. Or a circular saw. Because of this I sometimes place the entire empty bag into the garage, which is attached to the basement. When spring cleaning makes it to the garage I am in big trouble. The garage already has her mad because it s fairly narrow and does not allow much clearance on either side as you drive a car through the doorway. Furthermore, the door is heavy and must be opened manually. So, I use the garage for my truck, which makes loading the dogs to run rabbits much easier than leashing them and taking them to the curb.

So, she never goes in the garage. When she does, it is to clean and threaten harm to my fishing poles, hunting boots, clay pigeons, orange hats, and empty dog food bags.

The weight circles on the basement freezer are bad enough. Entire bags (from days when I emptied the new bags into the plastic feed bins and did not have a knife to remove the circle) enrage her. I thought of a great plan in the fall to mitigate her ire. I found a plastic cabinet in the house that was empty and put it in the garage. I have folded the empty bags and placed them in there. She will not even see the dog food bags before I remove the circles and redeem them for goodies and discounts.

The last problem for spring cleaning is my rabbit hunting gear. I keep the backseat of my truck full of every needed bit of hunting garb. Warm coats, briar-proof coats, insulated gloves, thin leather gloves, brush pants, brush-chaps, rubber boots, and heavy boots are stowed neatly on the fold down backseats of my *Dakota*. Shotgun shells of every gauge are tucked into the console and glove box. Leashes are scattered across the back of my truck the way stuffed animals clutter the back seats of a car owned by a soccer mom with little kids. Eventually, as the rabbit season ends, all of this gear makes its way into the house. By into the house, I mean about four feet into the house.

I will be reminded that this equipment needs to be stored properly every day until spring cleaning. At that point, I will be threatened to move it or lose it. But hey, I got it under control this year. I have been grooming the beagles. I have even moved some of the hunting gear from the truck and into summer storage. What could go wrong? I thin--wait a minute... My wife is yelling something from the basement. Hold on. Apparently, the cabinet in the garage was purchased for her scrapbook and card making supplies. I didn't know that. She says it has been "missing." I knew where it was. I hope she doesn't look inside that thing. I gotta go!

EVERGREENS

One of my fondest Christmas memories dates back to when I was in seminary, at The Methodist Theological School in Ohio, and I was working for the maintenance staff. I was a member of a rare and endangered species. This endangered species was a small group of people that might have been called young clergy, or at least future clergy. I had gone directly from high school to college, and then to seminary. I am rapidly approaching forty years of age, and forty may have been young for a seminarian at the time. As a twenty-two year old I was nearly the youngest student there. New pastors tend to be in their second or third career.

Youngsters like me, who were strong and able-bodied, tended to find themselves employed in the maintenance department. This was a combination custodial and general fix-it-up position. Those with more aptitude for repair were allowed to actually fix things. Those who demonstrated less know how were relegated to scrubbing and cleaning. By all rights I should have been scrubbing and cleaning, but the full-time guys liked me, and I got to go on repairs with Earl, who was the guy responsible for most of the actually *bona fide* repairs.

Earl loved Christmas lights, and he demonstrated this passion by lighting up our campus with a gigantic glow on every bush, tree, building, and street light. There were times that I feared small planes, piloted by guys with a private license, might mistake our campus roads for runways and land. All the lights were white, and there was a genuine brightness to everything. We even decorated the pine tree in front of the administrative building. The tree was over two stories high, and we had a less than safe way to wrap it in lights: We leaned two long ladders against it, and sent two guys up the ladder with long hooks while everyone else stabilized the base of the steeply angled aluminum roofing ladders. In the years that I was a student, I was always chosen to go up the tree. Eric Raygor, another Pennsylvania guy usually climbed the other ladder, and we would spiral the lights downward with the long hooks until they were accessible to the ground workers holding twelve foot poles. People stood around and watched, certain we would plummet to an untimely demise.

It takes a lot of lights to cover even a small campus, and this is where one of my great Christmas memories comes flooding to the forefront of my mind. We stored hundreds of Christmas light strings in the barn, each string rolled tight and tucked into a box, with many similar wound balls of festive lights stacked upon one another. We accepted donations of white lights, and even bought a few after Christmas, when the price was real low, for use the following year. The donated lights were often not fully operational—some section of the string was dead. The older lights, which had been stretched out and wound tight multiple times, suffered even more problems. Our solution was a device that I am not sure is actually available for purchase. It may be something that a clever troubleshooter invented. It was a box that was plugged into an electrical outlet, and then a string of Christmas bulbs could be plugged into the box. As soon as you plugged the lights into the contraption, they would turn on, just like plugging them into a normal outlet, revealing which lights were "broken" and therefore needed to be corrected. A lone bulb often indicated a single bad filament. Frequently the lights would work until they reached a certain point—maybe midway or less, and then every bulb after that was dark. This was indicative of a broken wire.

At this point was where the contraption found its real value. It had a button that could be depressed. Depressing the button always yielded a "zzzt" sound and the accompanying odor of ozone. The noise and odor was generated by the contraption surging electricity into the string of lights, effectively welding the broken wires back together. One or two depressions of the button for one or two seconds each, and the whole string would be resurrected for another year of peace on earth and good will towards men. But you could hold the button indefinitely. It was the male end of the plug that went into the contraption. The great fun was if you could depress the button that soldered the wires while someone was holding the female end of the string, because despite the plastic insulation a little spark would emerge from the end and give the guy holding it a jolt. This worked best the first time that someone ever held that end of the string, but provided even more delight when you could occasionally zap someone who knew better. It was silly, juvenile fun. I laughed with fits of mirth every time someone got the shock. Whenever I was victimized, however, I could not understand what was so funny.

Christmas tree farms are some of my favorite hunting places, and they are typically banned between Thanksgiving and Orthodox Christmas, as this is when people will browse the many acres of 3-8 foot trees looking for just the right specimen for their home. There are lots of Orthodox Christians in Pennsylvania, so the farms still have tree shoppers into the first week of January. I suppose the blasting of shotguns and the barking of beagles is bad for business, and I have to abandon these havens of bunnies for the holidays. I have always had great success hunting tree farms, and my old rabbit wise dogs love the ease of chasing in the groves of pines and spruce. I haven't been to Yankee Lake Beagle Club in many years, but I know they would typically host their trials on a Christmas tree farm. My dogs would walk from one tree to the next, sniffing under each until a rabbit was flushed. They had learned this practice from hunting similar tree farms, and a seasoned beagle looks like a slalom skier as it goes down one row of evergreens and up the next, hunting for the many rabbits that tend to sit directly under the trees and are often reluctant to run until they are almost bumped by the nose of a beagle.

In much of Appalachia, the old strip mines often utilized evergreens to reclaim the land after the coal was excavated. The old surface mines never have the deep layer of topsoil that was present before the coal was removed, and the shallow roots of little pine trees do well in those conditions. Usually they are planted in rows akin to an actual tree farm, and it is in these places that I often hunt while the domesticated tree farms are off limits. And it is in the pines that I often ambush hunt. The basic premise of ambush hunting rabbits is based upon my father's adage that "Statues shoot rabbits."

What he meant was that a smart hunter finds a place to wait for the rabbit and attempts to stand as still as possible. There are few things I like more than the opportunity to tumble a rabbit as it is crossing a wide dirt road. In reality, this seldom happens because the rabbit will approach the edge of the brushy cover and then turn in a new direction, never crossing the road. I also like to be in open clearings that may pepper vast stretches of goldenrod. Here again the rabbit generally never emerges into the clearing , but rather hugs the perimeter of the thick cover affording no opportunity to see the rodent as it sneaks and streaks past the most statuesque hunter.

I developed ambush hunting in red brush, but it works equally well in little groves of evergreen trees. A cunning cottontail might be sticking to a single patch of trees and never crossing any open ground. I typically wade into the cover and look for an intersection of rabbit trails. The rabbit trails rarely provide much visibility, which is precisely why the rabbits are using them. They are great places to avoid the air predators that could easily find a rabbit in an open field or dirt road. This lack of visibility is often remedied by kneeling. Sometimes I will even sit with my feet underneath me and this position places me under the canopy of cover and concealment. A good intersection will have several escape routes converging under the hunter. This is where I set up my ambush, and the most important part of ambush hunting is to not look for rabbits, but rather to remain statue still listen for the hippity-hoppity sounds as the rabbit weaves through the cover. Once I hear the rabbit I will slowly pivot to face the trails that are in that direction. I call this method ambush hunting because as soon as I see the rabbit and mount the gun to my shoulder the rabbit will frequently stop stark still, having been caught off guard by a human sitting down in the middle of a bunch of pine trees. After you squeeze the trigger the last step to complete a successful ambush hunt is to stretch out your legs and pray that your feet, which have fallen asleep by now, will awake in time for you to go retrieve the rabbit before your pack of beagles devour the bunny.

Ambush hunting is also when I pick out my favorite little Christmas tree. My wife has converted me to an artificial tree, which does not provide nearly as much fun as a real tree. When I say fun, I mean the great joy of searching the tree for mice and other vermin that may have nests inside, repeatedly rotating the tree in every configuration to see which side is the fullest, adding water to it every few days, and stepping on sharp needles in your stocking feet until Easter. But there is no scent from an artificial tree, although I am sure someone is working on that problem. So I am permitted, after much begging, to bring a small live tree into the house. Or, I should say, a recently live tree. I often pick one near an ambush spot. When you sit on your feet for twenty minutes at a time you get great opportunities to see a potential Christmas tree from many angles.

I usually pick one about four feet high. That height is just right for holding a bunny, which is why I cannot keep the thing on the floor, because my beagles keep nosing around under it looking for rabbits. So my little tree sits on a folding, wooden table that has two leafs which fold downward. This little table sits in storage most of the year, its primary purpose being to hold desserts at Thanksgiving. It is basically a glorified card playing table, but it works perfect for my little tree. All of the decorations on this tree are beagles. When you are known as "The Pastor with the beagles" people tend to buy beagle ornaments for you, and I actually have enough to decorate the entire tree. This, of course, begs the question "Do you use a star or an angel on the top?" The answer is I use a Santa. More accurately, I use a toy stuffed animal of a beagle wearing a Santa cap. I tie it to the top with 4 lb. test invisible fishing line. The little puppy appears to be hovering in mid-air.

And this creates the perfect table for alternative gifts for the beagler. What kind of gifts? Well, things you may not think that a person may need, and so I will give you a list. These are great gift ideas for the beagler in your life! First, is left handed gloves. I have never been able to feel comfortable shooting with gloves. I bite my right glove off my hand whenever I see deer from my tree stand, and I refuse to wear a right glove when I am small game hunting. I hold the cold barrel in my gloved left hand while small game hunting, keeping my right hand on the wooden stock so as to remain a bit warmer. There was a time when I would place the right glove in my vest pocket, and then that glove would get lost. This is expensive if you buy good gloves! Do the beagler in your life a favor, and collect unmatched left handed gloves all year long, and leave them in his or her stocking. Nothing is better than putting your hand into a big sock and finding a bunch of gloves. I suppose if your beagler is left handed then you will need to get right handed gloves.

A beagler can never have too many leashes. Some places make them five feet long. A nice five foot lead goes diagonal over the shoulder nicely, and has that extra twelve inches of give to accommodate extra shirts, coats, a hunting vest, and ten extra pounds of belly. A five foot lead will make you happier! Also, while you are at it, go ahead and pick up a coupler that consists of an O ring and two snaps. These are great for tying a dog to a sapling, or temporarily fastening a prized pooch to the tailgate cable as you get water poured for Fido. I have also attached one end to the lead and the other to my belt loop on a few instances when my hands were full. A coupler is never bad to carry in the event that you have to catch a friend's dog and you only have one lead.

A big bag of socks should go under the special beagle tree too. First, if you have house beagles that are puppies, then you may be low on socks. Second, there is no greater treat in the world after first series at a trial, or before lunch while hunting, than the simple act of changing socks and getting your feet dry. Sometimes rubber boots keep your feet dry from the dew but wet from sweat. A bag of socks in the back of your pickup truck's cab is a luxury beyond words. Some heavy socks for winter season are a nice bonus as well.

GPS is expensive for a dog, but a bell is cheaper. I use bells on my beagles to protect them from unsafe hunters and to know where my dogs are when they are not barking. Lion Country Supply sells a little bell for bird dogs (I think they are the primary customers of the bells) that is small enough for a beagle and I can hear it for 100 yards under ideal conditions. Where guys with pointers listen for the bell to go silent, indicating the dog is on point, I can tell when the dog is about to jump a rabbit because the bell gets louder and faster just before he opens in full cry on a hot line. It is *Lion Country's* most expensive bell, but it is worth it. Just a word of caution, after your dogs get accustomed to wearing the bell, you will be able to incite them to rabbit fever by jingling it, so keep the bells in the truck—they can stay excited for quite some time on a mistaken bell rattling that is not followed by rabbits. Pavlov was more right than he knew—no dog wants food as bad as a beagle wants a rabbit.

Lastly, I will mention *Polywad*. They are an ammunition company that makes spreader loads. The wad causes the shot to expand much faster than usual, and the end result is that even a mediocre shotgunner can enjoy great success when blasting a running rabbit. Hitting more rabbits is always a gift, and wounding less rabbits always makes me happy. The first time I patterned the shells made by *Polywad* rounds I was amazed. They have a website, and a box or two of their shells in your favorite gauge is a wonderful gift. They make shells chambered in 2½" to fit those old guns too.

Well, times are tough all over, and I hope these gift ideas will make you a hit when it comes to gifts for beaglers. A warm left hand and dry feet make me comfortable in the field, and knowing where my dogs are and more rabbits in the freezer makes me happier when I go home. I am going to leave this article for my wife to read, just in case she is looking for gift ideas for me. Oh, and I have a stand of pine trees to visit to get my Christmas tree. Pennsylvania is known for Christmas tree farms. I have even heard that the big tree that sits in front of the white house has come from Pennsylvania in the past. Do you suppose they use a couple hillbilly seminarians to decorate it?

YOU'RE WELCOME, SANTA

Well, it was bound to happen sooner or later—I confronted Santa on his home turf. My long term readers will be aware that Santa has asked several favors from me over the years--mostly in the realm of delivering Christmas presents for him, due to cowardice. You see, Pennsylvania is known as a state that takes deer hunting seriously, and Saint Nicholas is occasionally worried about the prospect of flying his caribou over the Keystone State. I mean, there is no game law protecting reindeer like the laws that ensure safety for Pennsylvania's wild elk herd in Elk County. Those particular semi-tame hoofed animals can only be shot if you win the elk lottery, wherein the game commission makes a boat load of money to issue a few tags. There is, as far as I know, no laws pertaining to caribou per se, other than maybe a catch all clause somewhere. Santa knows that it is impossible for antlers that big could fly over some parts of my home state without receiving AAA fire from various and assorted 30 caliber rifles, therefore he sometimes has found me in early December and procured a little assistance.

It turns out that I was at the North Pole in September. Ironically, the North Pole is not at the North Pole, but rather it is a few miles from Fairbanks Alaska. I was there for the Outdoor Writers Association of America's annual meeting. It turns out that fat elf has a hospitality streak, and his house is well advertised and open to the public. Just be aware, you will have to pay money for anything you eat or drink at his store-like abode. Ditto for any souvenirs you want to bring home. Apparently he only gives stuff away on December 24th. At any rate, he was nonchalantly talking with someone else while I was in ear shot, "So, the outdoor writers are here for a week," he chuckled with pleasure while eating a cookie to maintain his jolly figure (it takes year round training) "Apparently Alaska will receive 30 million in free advertising as a result."

"Oh yeah?" his conversation partner said, "How so?"

"Well, they will all go home and write stories about their Alaskan adventures, and that should draw people to the area," the saint explained.

"Really?" I chimed in, "That is something."

Santa looked at me and seemed to recognize my face, "Do I know you, Sir?"

"Yep, I got the botched Star Wars order under the tree in 1981," I explained, "And due to your awareness of the legendary marksmanship abilities of Pennsylvanians, dating back to the Buck Tail Brigade, you had me deliver some toys a few years back."

"Yes, yes, good to see you, Pastor! Say, you are a writer, won't you help Alaska?"

"Sure!" I exclaimed, "And no worries on the 1981 debacle, I know how mistakes can happen. You can make it up to me this year. I'd like a camper for my truck—the kind that sits in the bed-- to go on long hunting trips. You can put it under the big pine tree in the yard. I will throw a few lights on it so you know which one."

Santa said the same thing he has said since I was a kid, "We will see how good you are." It doesn't look good for me.

I left the North Pole feeling a need to detail something unique about Alaska. So, hear goes.....

Upon registering for the writer's conference I was immediately inundated with literature advertising things that were free—or greatly reduced in price—for us members of OWAA. One of the things promoted was a free trip to the Aurora Borealis lodge for the purpose of viewing the Northern Lights. My wife and I decided to try and see the lights on the night of our anniversary, Sept 2. The lodge is perfect, and sits atop a hill that is not much higher than the peaks of Pennsylvania—relatively flatland in Alaska. A dirt road snakes to the top of the hill, and the lodge has a gorgeous sitting room with the biggest picture window I have ever seen facing the northern sky. The window overlooks a deck, where viewing is even better without the barrier of glass. The lodge did offer sleeping accommodations in a neighboring building, but we were going to try and see the lights and head back to the hotel we rented until the conference began.

The only other light seekers besides us were about 40 Japanese tourists. The owner of the lodge spoke fluent Japanese, so my wife and I missed much of the conversation, all most all of it, in fact. People took turns going out to the observation deck to see the lights, as a faint aurora would not be visible from inside the glass.

"How will we know if they see lights?" Renee asked.

"We will know," I said, fighting sleep on the couch. It was midnight AK time but it felt like 4 a.m. to me, "There will be no translation necessary for "OOOOH" I explained.

I was wrong. There was no translator required for "AWWWWW!" We all rushed onto the deck, and there we saw an amazing light display. Actually, it wasn't all that amazing by Alaskan standards. To me, however, it was the greatest glimpse of the lights that I had ever stood under, especially since the only other time that I have seen the magical cosmic light show was at the Rolfe Beagle Club when I was a kid. The local news back then had indicated that there was a slight chance of viewing the lights that winter evening, even in the Mid-Atlantic States, due to very high solar activity, which is what causes the actual aurora. We did see the lights—a very faint red glow that almost looked like the lights of a town, and the display was very brief. By comparison the green streaks in Fairbanks were a world class laser show, although it was quite mediocre by northern standards.

The owner of the Aurora Borealis Lodge is a very accomplished photographer, and he took a few pictures of Renee and me for our anniversary. The process of standing for these pictures resembles posing in an old west black powder photo because you have to stand still for four seconds—that is how long the shutter is open. On the last second or so he shines a light on the people so that they too are visible under the lights. It is a rather spectacular souvenir, and with the OWAA discount it was only a few bucks. We departed for our hotel feeling happy, but exhausted.

Many of the outdoor writers are also photographers who tried to get a photo of the northern lights, but few were able due to overcast conditions for most of the week. It seems that we took advantage of the best night throughout the whole week we were in Alaska. The conference was held at Chena Hot Springs, an hour's drive from Fairbanks. Driving an hour in Alaska is like driving 5 minutes in most places, sometimes Alaskans drive for days to get to a hunting spot. Chena Hot Springs has a building up on a hill called an Aurorium—it is designed just for viewing the lights. We went up there one night with some other writers to try and see (and photograph, of course) the Northern Lights.

People decided to go in a group due to a concern for grizzlies. Indeed, there were warning signs all over the Hot Springs resort warning of this danger. We decided to walk in a talkative huddle for safety. No one wanted to lead the way up the twisting trail that led to the glass encased building at the top of the hill.

"Alright," I said, deciding to be point man "I will lead the way. I have a .22 pistol for protection from the bears."

"A .22?" another fellow asked, "What will that do?"

"A lot," I said, "We may as well decide now who I should shoot in the knee in the event we run into a ravenous bear gorging for winter. Who wants it?"

"He's a humor writer," my mentor Ty explained.

"Not a funny one," came the response.

"I have no gun," I confessed, "Flying with a gun is too much hassle. I was worried that there might be one shotgun shell in my luggage from a hunting trip and airport security would find it and arrest me."

"Did that happen?" Ty asked.

"Nah, worse. They found a six ounce container of shampoo. I was almost probed in the airport."

I began eyeing one writer who looked to be a slower runner than me, and deciding to stick close to him on the walk—I only had to outrun one of these guys. I am actually good at finding the slow runners—I was always the second to last kid picked for games in gym class, and I can quickly locate the fellow that was last in his school. We arrived at the Aurorium in time to watch the sky get socked in with clouds. People set up cameras, and we walked inside the warm building to chat and wait for the skies to clear. They never did clear until morning. The conversation quickly turned to the topic of despair caused by sunny daylight hours and cloudy skies every night.

"Here is our picture," I said while whipping out my phone and searching for the photo that the Aurora Borealis Lodge had emailed us. Everyone was quite impressed, and we narrated the story of the 40 Japanese tourists who had to be shuttled up to the lodge because their bus was too long for the serpentine dirt lane.

"Yeah, stay out of the geothermal pools at night when the tourists are here from Japan," Someone said, "That is what they told us." She chuckled.

"What?" I asked.

"You don't know? Ever wonder why there are signs in Japanese everywhere in Alaska?"

"Hey, there are too," I said, "Why?"

"They plan their vacations here to get pregnant, because in their culture it is believed that a child conceived under the northern lights will be very intelligent and gifted."

I suddenly remembered Santa's conversation with me a few days earlier, and the need to bring tourist money to Alaska. But I write for beagle magazines, how could I help? Well, here is the plan. I would like to return to Alaska, perhaps for several months each year. There is, naturally, lots of big game to hunt there, but snowshoe hare are plentiful as well. I have seen pictures of great hare hunts with beagles in the northernmost state. Beagles, of course would be essential to this work of hunting hare when I am not chasing sheep, caribou, bear and moose. This brings me to the next phase of the plan.

I would need a small lodge there, equipped with kennels. A quick perusal of the fees associated with hunting the 49th state reveals the harsh reality that I lack the necessary income to get this accomplished. I mean it is expensive! Field trials, however, are big business. The pursuit of field champions is what drives our sport, and then all the stud fees that follow. The only problem is determining which pup will be a field champion. Do you

line breed? How about an outcross? What if you breed a
hare proven bitch with a cottontail veteran sire, or vice
versa? How do you ensure field champions?

No worries, I can solve your problems. You can breed
to my male beagles, which I might add, are proven hunters.
No, they don't have any ribbons, trophies, or titles, but
that is irrelevant. You see, I will take my stud dogs to
Alaska. You send me your female in estrus. When the
lights come out, I put your bitch with any one of my male
dogs (your choice). It won't matter which stud you pick,
the lights will take care of it. Imagine this—instead of one,
gifted, baby child conceived under the expansive light show
and arriving in 9 months; we could have a whole litter of
amazingly gifted pups that will emerge in roughly 60 days,
all of them future field champions! Just think of the
money you could charge for these pups. Of course, I would
have to charge you a hefty fee as well. It is a hell of a
sacrifice I am willing to make for you—moving to Alaska a
few months each year to hunt and also breed your dogs,
but hey, I am a giving person. Since the dogs have to
breed under the lights for the full effect, I will have to hunt
all day and wait till dark to ensure gifted offspring. Big
game of course is my goal, but I will hunt hare as well. So
if any of you have field champion males that you want me
to put at stud I can do that too. We will split the stud fee.
The stud fee will be twice what I charge for my dogs—yours
are champions, after all. I will also hunt over your field
champions during the day so that you can brag of their
success in the wilds of Alaska. You will have amazing
progeny records as a result. AKC will be impressed beyond
belief at the producing power of your field champion stud.
No one else, of course, need know about the lights. When I
return your stud to you, following my hunts, there will still
be a demand for your pooch's services. This is because
word will spread that every litter sired by your stud in
those early autumn months was packed full of field
champions. I am surprised that no geneticist has
stumbled onto this strategy in the past. I figure I should
be able to afford to hire great guides, rent a small plane
with a pilot, and eat at some nice restaurants in the cities.
All of this amounts to money flowing into Alaska as a

result of my writing. I am a little worried that this means I will be working in the sex industry. I will not be offering souvenir pictures under the lights. That is too far down the wrong road. But I really want that camper for hunting the lower 48 states. You're Welcome, Santa.

TROPHY HUSBAND

I stepped into my yard the other day to view the carnage of winter. The snow had melted, and I was able to see the short, pale, yellow grass that is a shadow of its former self. Strewn throughout the yard were all the dog toys that I bought when my two puppies were whelped last summer. I sold all the puppies except one, well almost. I sold one puppy twice, but he ended up staying here. The first buyer sent a deposit and never called back. The second buyer paid for the dog and then had to move from a house into an apartment, and so I bought the pup back. There was a third opportunity, but by that time the pup was housebroke, and more importantly, sleeping on the couch with my wife during the evening news. At that point the pup was clearly part of our pack of hunting house hounds. This was all occurring during the late summer and early fall.

In addition to all the dog toys, there were various missing items that the melted snow had revealed. Socks in large numbers, a belt, a guitar strap, a pair of my favorite slippers. Each mate of the pair went missing on separate occasions, but both now lie in opposite corners of the fenced lawn, like two fighters waiting for the bell. Every item that had gone missing over the winter was evidently kidnapped into the yard by the two pups that have spent almost all of their time since being weaned playing tug-of-war with each other. They will play this favorite game with absolutely anything they can get their teeth on. One of their favorite choices is a pair of underwear or some other undergarment stolen from the hamper. Such prized tug-of-war materials are the equivalent of a game ball in football or some other sport—never utilized in practice and only brought out for the main event. The main event occurs whenever we have company, especially church members. That is when the *Fruit-of-the-Loom* game ball makes its appearance; and the two pups square off for fake growls and wild maneuvers as they tumble and roll through the kitchen trying to gain the upper hand on one another. Typically one will perform a crocodile death roll with the underwear tightly gripped in his teeth right at the guest's feet.

Most of the parishioners who come to the house are church members in the parish my wife serves—I have to commute 40 miles to the churches where I work, so at least most of the embarrassment of crude puppies belongs to Renee! Anyway, I was cleaning the mess in the yard, and the rake scraped across the concrete moat that I installed last summer to prevent the pint-sized (then) pups from escaping under the fence. That was a hot, muggy, miserable summer day with no breeze whatsoever. I mixed the ready mix cement in a bucket with a hose. I was wearing my favorite blue jeans, which incidentally are full of holes. I also had my favorite t-shirt, which incidentally is about worn out but has a great picture of a beagle on it. I was as comfortable as I could be in the heat, but was anxious to get the hole plugged before the puppies next scheduled visit into the yard. My beard was longer and more unkempt than normal, no doubt streaked with concrete from the repeated act of wiping sweat away. My arms were likewise grey with fast-drying cement.

Apparently, someone had been knocking on the door to the house and decided to let themselves in. The gentleman walked through our house and out into the backyard where I was working.

"Hello?" I said, turning to greet the gentleman. Cement covered my tattered clothing.

"Is the pastor here?" He said.

"How can I help you?" I responded.

"I was looking for the pastor, are you her husband?" he queried.

"Oh," I exclaimed, realizing he meant the other pastor who lived here, "I am her husband. She is out right now, anything I can do?"

"I see. I never met you before," he sized me up taking notice of my ripped jeans and concrete beard, "and just what do you do for a living?"

It is worth mentioning that I really don't like this question when it appears in small-talk between strangers. We instantly make judgments on people based on what we do for a living and where we work, and I find that to be somewhat unfortunate. I could have told the man that I was a pastor, or a part-time college teacher, as they are both true. Instead I responded with, "You're lookin' at what I do, mister." He pulled his head back and widened his eyes in disbelief. I continued, "Yessir, I mostly look after the yard and house and other than that my job is mostly loookin' good and being eye candy for the Mrs."

"Really?" was the only response he could mutter.

"Yep. You've heard of trophy wives? Well I am trophy husband through and through!" I raised my shirt and pushed my belly out to look bigger as I patted it with my right hand.

"I'll stop back later," The visitor said, and let himself out. He never did give his name.

I finished cleaning the springtime yard, chuckling to myself as I remembered that event from last summer. It's even funnier now, because my wife will call me a "trophy husband" in public as a joke. I'm an average looking dude, and that adds to the humor. Oh well, I guess you just can't judge a book by its cover.

Take my puppies for instance, they still tumble around the house fighting over anything they can find, but in the woods they are starting to take an interest in rabbits. Perhaps they will become trophy beagles. Well, I guess ribbon-beagles would be the more accurate term in our sport. Hey, it could happen. Every puppy is the very incarnation of pure hope. They might be those dogs that always make winners pack, never make a mistake in front of the judge, always jump the rabbit, always solve the tough check in front of the entire gallery. Yes, I can see it now.

Actually, what I see as I type this story are 8-month old beasts that are playing tug-of-war with a pair of underwear. The game ball is out, we must be getting company. I better go look for my favorite pants and t-shirt. Or, perhaps I should take the pups out to smell some more of the rabbits that have been gaining their attention. Sure,

my wife jokes about the trophy husband comment now,
but she had to explain it to her parishioner who found me
in the yard. It took her a few months to see the humor.

TRAP LINES

Heretofore my most successful trap line was in my childhood, when my local beagle club paid kids to release box trapped rabbits into the running pen. That was a club that had very few people running dogs, most of the members owning traditional brace hounds. That was not a bad thing, as those of us with gundogs had the running grounds to ourselves, and kids made a few dollars per rabbit due to the need to have massive amounts of rabbits in order to finish a trial with brace dogs. This was in the 80's (or, way back in the 1900's as my step-son says) and the brace trialing crowd had slow, no-hunt, pottering dogs as they do now, but they still enjoyed a larger number of entries than the same trials do today. From what I gather, it takes a great deal of wins to finish a brace hound today because of the low entries—I can envision 12+ wins necessary to get the required champion points! There are more vehicles at a small church choir practice than there are in the parking lot of a traditional brace trial—and half the cars at the trial are people who showed up to cook the food for the judges and the other two guys who brought dogs.

As I remember, back then, they never cast hounds to search. Instead, skirmish lines of men brandishing sawed off golf clubs found the rabbits by driving the brush, marching in formation until a rabbit was scared out onto one of the many feed strips that were mowed for such occasions. When a rabbit emerged the entire gallery erupted in "Tally-Ho" fanfare as if the last rabbit on earth had been located, and brace hounds were carried by their owners to the marked line where the handlers fumbled with their leashes, each trying to release their hound last in order to secure the coveted "back position." It took a lot of rabbits to run these trials, and I relished the chance to live trap the yard dwelling cottontails to make some cash during the winter months.

The only other trap lines which I have ever managed were in the church. Old churches are less than weatherproof, and every autumn the field mice find a way into the buildings and feast on the varieties of treats found there—crumbs left by the various children who arrive at worship with little sandwich bags of dry, sugar coated breakfast cereal, morsels left on counters after Sunday school, or whatever. Bible studies always have snacks. Sometimes the mice even manage to chew through the cardboard and paper containers of chips and ready mix scalloped potatoes that are always found in church kitchens. I begin trapping after the first frost, and by Christmas the onslaught of heat seeking rodents are gone. Peanut butter is my favorite mouse bait—it is sufficiently sticky that the varmints have to gnaw with enough pressure to trigger the trap. I normally set the traps after evening meetings or Bible studies, and return early so as to dispose of the buggers without anyone noticing.

I was not married when I arrived at the parish I now serve, and I do not eat much peanut butter. So, when I saw evidence of a mouse that first autumn, I rushed to the local grocery store to buy a jar. Coincidentally, our church was helping a family for Christmas, and at the beginning of advent a tree was decorated with ornaments. Each ornament was made of foam rubber and cut in the shape of a candle or tree or candy cane or some other Christmas shape. Written on each was an item to be purchased to help the local family. Church members grabbed a foam rubber ornament and returned the prescribed gift (wrapped, of course) by the Sunday before Christmas. For instance, a decoration might read "boots, boy, size 6" or "toy, girl, age 8." Every child got toys, clothes and boots. My decoration simply read "diapers."

While buying peanut butter for the mice, I also bought diapers for the advent family. One of the elderly women of the church saw me in the store and was perplexed at the presence of diapers in an unmarried pastor's shopping cart, and it caused quite a ruckus. I was the talk of the town until it got sorted out. I intentionally left the diapers unwrapped when I placed them under the advent gift tree in the sanctuary—I didn't think the baby would care. It was big church gossip.

Recently, I have joined a beagle club—a former brace club that once forbade guys like me but has had a conversion to the gundog side of the force. It is a member of the Pennsylvania Beagle Gundog Association, and runs two licensed gundog trials per year in addition to the sanctioned and association trials. I am box trapping rabbits once again to help the club, only there is no pay. My endeavor is to help create elite athletes. Let me explain. The average yard rabbit, or wild rabbit for that matter, is not a professional athlete. They rarely run in front of dogs. This is plain enough to notice when we hunt, as the rabbits tend to run in big, squared circles without trying very many tricks to lose the beagles. Oftentimes the pressure of the chase will force these amateur bunnies underground. Professional rabbits, by contrast, are the ones that nonchalantly chew clover in the open as you drive to the running grounds, and then watch as you proceed to release your hounds from the bed of the truck. At this point the professional may run into the brush and try some tricks, or if it s a particularly confident rabbit, it may wait for the hounds so as to incite a sight chase before it dodges into the thickest cover to await the results—some beagles become so excited from seeing the rodent that they never recover!

Professional rabbits love to run spaghetti strands instead of circles, and delight in doubles or even triples on the checks. They quickly learn the poor scenting areas of their territory and will make frequent trips over the shale and bone dry dirt to stall or delay the dogs. There are rewards for the elite bunnies, the corn and feed pellets are in abundance throughout the winter, and cover could not be better at many beagle clubs. In fact, I have been in clubs that have brush piles sufficiently large as to be analogous to a hole in the ground in terms of ending chases. I have always feared these professional rabbits when training puppies, but admire them for their raw trickery and running ability. A few months of training in a beagle club and the state game land rabbits of November are no problem for a rabbit-wise hound.

Apples and apple juice have always been my lure of choice for live trapping bunnies. Apples in the box, juice around it. In fact, I will let you in on a little secret—I have better luck with apple juice from the baby food section of the grocery store. I stumbled on to this by accident. I was a teenager trapping rabbits in my cousin's yard when my spray bottle of juice was out of the sweet ammunition that I utilize to saturate the interior of the box trap and the ground immediately before the entrance. I burst into my cousin Marsha's house in a state of dejection, and she reached into the refrigerator and produced a bottle of apple juice that was made by *Gerber*. I am not sure what is in the baby juice, or perhaps the allure may be what is not added, but it has always worked better for me. Perhaps it is coincidence and the juice is actually identical to the product intended for adults. But I use baby apple juice.

As you read these words the trapping season will be over and I will be running inside the fence now and again, although I still enjoy the old logging cuts and reclaimed strip mines that are closer to home. For now, as I type, there is a little time left to procure some professional athletes from the yards in town. Hmmm....I wonder what those elderly church ladies will think when they see me buying apple juice in the baby aisle? At least I am married now. I sure hope no one asks my wife if she is pregnant. She will not like that question.

ILLNESSES THAT BEAGLERS MUST AVOID

Have you noticed that there seems to be no limit of things to worry about these days? This is especially true for the outdoorsman. Why, every time I turn around I find a new medical worry. For instance, let me tell you about a polite, enthusiastic beagler (me) trying to spot the credits and faults in his dogs.

My youngest hound is about three years old. I was always cautious about running him with the rest of the pack when he was younger because I did not want him to get beat all the time. I fear that a young dog that gets beat all the time will not develop to potential, and probably will develop bad habits. You may disagree with me there, but please understand that this assumption is crucial to what happens next. You see, I *used* to worry about my young dog gaining bad habits from being beaten. Now, I am starting to worry that the young fella is putting some real moves on his packmates, and one of the more experienced hounds is--I think--stealing the front of the pack by running the first bit of a line from a check mute. The "pup" is beating the older dogs. I wanted to see if this was true, so I started trying to watch more of the chase.

Watching the chase necessarily means running hard after the hounds. Don't get me wrong, I can't keep up with them, but I can get in front of the dogs and see the check work. My problem is that I did not belong to a beagle club when this happened. If you have read my column in the past, then you realize that I am surrounded by old brace clubs, none of which would let me join. There are some gundog clubs about, but I am an hour and a half away. So, I run in places that are not maintained. This means that there are no mowed paths. Say what you want about those blasted mowed paths--I know that they can cause grief--

but they also allow you to get good views of the bunny and hounds too.

So, there I was trying to see what I can see, running through multifloral rose and greenbriar and tall grass and weeds, bouncing off dead logs and hidden tree trucks. I routinely returned looking like a bear mauled me, all flesh covered in briar scratches. I walked in the house bleeding.

"Where have you been?" My wife asked

"Trying to see the dogs on check. I think I have a cheater."

"Oh, can you see it?" She asked.

"No...not really...maybe...it is just so thick in that brush."

"What is that smell?" she asked, sniffing the air, "are you wearing after shave in the woods? You don't even shave!"

"It's deet."

"What?"

"Deet, you know, bug juice. The gnats are torture out there."

"Isn't that stuff carcinogenic?" she squinted at me concerned.

"I dunno. I guess I need some cancer causing chemicals since I don't smoke."

When I got up the next morning to try and see the hounds I found that my Deet had been replaced by a less potent bug repellent, made by a cosmetics company. I guess it was my better half's way of trying to keep me from getting cancer. Cute, in a way. That is until I got in the woods and was thoroughly covered in bug bites. I lost track of the dogs I was bitten so badly. I ran into things and bounced around the woods. I left the woods looking like I was 13 years old with the worst case of acne ever reported.

I walked in the house scratching and itching.

"Oh my God," My dear wife said when she saw me, clasping her hands over her mouth and eyes in horror, "What happened?"

"Don't worry about cancer," I said, "I won't live long enough to get it. I think I am several pints low on blood from all these bug bites."

"You aren't low on blood, and at least you are safe from the chemicals."

"Yeah, but I probably have Lyme Disease and West Nile both." I joked.

That is when my wife's jaw dropped and she began to have way too many worries about the matter.

"Look," I explained," I have no tick bites at all, and for all we know I could have had the West Nile thing before. The newspaper said that most people who get the West Nile Disease don't even know it--it looks like the flu or even more mild."

Well. That didn't help. She insisted on worrying about diseases. The good thing is that the deet reappeared, and in several forms too. I had bug spray enough to last years. Then when we had a cookout and I noticed a bug-bite like bruise on my leg. The discoloration grew. There was a black and flesh-colored ring around it. It took over a large part of my thigh. My wife called me into the study to look at the computer and her internet discoveries.

"Honey," she said, "You either have Lyme disease or a brown recluse spider has bitten you and your leg tissue will die." She scrolled through a series of photos, each scarier than the previous, and each detailing the problems I would have. I could lose a limb with the spider bite, or the Lyme could ruin my nervous system. For days this kept me awake, or should I say for nights.

"It is just a bruise," I said.

"No, it's worse," Renee insisted.

"I would bet on it," I boomed confidently.

"We are Methodist Clergy, we don't gamble" was her response.

"It is just a black and blue mark," I repeatedly insisted, and it did look like a black and blue mark. I had banged my body off many stumps trying to catch the old veteran cheating on the chases. But the black and blue mark was big and awful colored and it grew quite large. Finally my wife's worry became infectious, and I was seized with all of her anxieties. One last nag from her and I raced off to the hospital.

"Can I help you?" the E.R. nurse asked.

"Yes, apparently I am dying from a bug bite."

"O.K." the nurse replied with skepticism in her voice, "What kind of bug bite do you have?"

"I dunno."

"So, how do you know that you are dying?"

"The same way that most men know things," I replied, "My wife told me." Said wife looked at me with a warning.

"Could you have a seat please?" the nurse instructed.

In short order the doctor came in and looked at my leg. "Ooh, that's a hematoma and a bad one too," he said.

"Good Lord," I thought silently to myself, "What the hell kind of a bug is a hematoma?"

"Oh, well my wife was sure it was Lyme disease or a brown recluse?" I said.

"Nope, it is a hematoma."

"How long do I have doc?"

"Ten days if you're lucky." I saw my life passing before my eyes. Ten days wasn't much life. I had too much that I wanted to do.

"You know what a hematoma is don't you?" the doc continued, "It is blood under the skin that ruptured and is trying to get out. Do some gently stretching and use warm heat and you can accelerate the healing process down to ten days. You're fine."

"Could I have gotten that bruise running into tree stumps and chasing dogs through the woods?"

"Absolutely. Why weren't you watching where you were running?"

"Too many bugs in my eyes, you know that gnats that go for the moisture in your eyes?"

"Well, you should use insect repellent in situations like that," the doctor said, scribbling notes for my discharge.

I looked over at my wife, the instigator of worry, she smiled and said, "Hooray, you're O.K."

"Say doc," I asked, "just to settle a friendly marital bet, how close was my layman's diagnosis of a 'black and blue mark'?"

"You were spot on." The doc winked and walked away.

"What do you mean bet, we didn't bet anything," My wife said.

"Sure we did. Maybe you can buy me gas for a week, or at least pay the co-pay on this hospital bill."

MID-LIFER

A mid-life crisis is not an event to be taken lightly. After all, these sorts of things can have a lasting impact. One of the certain realities about a midlife crisis is that the event can provide wonderful entertainment for those who might witness it. Moreover, it is worth noting, that the amount of enjoyment that a midlife crisis produces is directly proportional to the amount of money that the mid-lifer is willing to spend.

My friend, Dod, is on his third mid-life crisis. Each one has been absolutely fantastic for spectators. Dod's first mid-life crisis involved a farm. It was actually a venture that got taken over by his wife, who decided to grow pussy willows on a commercial basis. Apparently she felt that the market had more of a demand for pussy willows than really existed. An additional problem was created because she did not believe in hurting animals and the rabbits were destroying her cash crop. I was able to save the day with a few rigorous days of rabbit hunting, although my friend Lenny likes to point out that it really isn't that difficult to shoot rabbits on a piece of property that seems to have a dozen rabbits per acre. Lenny also says that it doesn't take much of a hound to be effective when the land has such a high rabbit density. All I have to say to Lenny is this: "Nanny nanny boo boo, you can't hunt where I do. Ha Ha Ha Ha."

Anyway, Dod's second midlife crisis took the form of a Harley Davidson. This was a radical departure from his other mode of transportation--a Buick Park Avenue. Dod kept the Buick, but he rode around on his Hog whenever he could. He especially liked to ride the Bike to his workplace. That daily commute provided him with 1.7 miles of utter, stop-and-go, 25 mph freedom. By the way, Dod is a dentist. He would cruise up to his office on his

Harley, wearing a suit and a brand new, Harley Davidson emblazoned leather jacket.

Dod also joined a motorcycle gang called "The Pros", short for the professionals. If you have priced a Harley recently, then you will see why many of the people riding these bikes are upper middle class, middle aged guys. The pros are a group of wealthy, pudgy, balding, guys who all ride Harley's together. Oftentimes they would ride in parades to support local charities. Sometimes the Shriners would harass the "Pros" with their moped-like vehicles. The mopeds had a tighter turning radius, and the Shriners took advantage of that fact to torment the Harley powered "Pros." When Dod's gang was not focused on such civic duty they rode around town in brand new leather jackets and full faced helmets, pausing on occasion to hang out at the local ice cream stand, ingesting no-fat yogurt like it was air. As you can gather, the "Pros" are a rather fierce gang. They do a lot of drugs together--all doctor prescribed for ailments like indigestion, constipation, diabetes, psoriasis, hemorrhoids, hypertension, and flatulence. The reason I know this is because these leading men of the community would sit in the local ice cream store parking lot and talk about their physical maladies. It was usually done in a rebellious fashion with a toothpick wedged between their front teeth (All but Dod--dentists do not abuse their teeth in that way). This was their great rebellion. They would sit in a very public place and discuss health concerns.

"I was on the toilet all day, yesterday," a banker would say as people walked by.

"Don't tell me your troubles," the local insurance guru would interrupt, "I have had gas for weeks now."

"Well," the local injury lawyer would chime in, "I am in litigation now because the drug store will not carry the brand of adult diapers that I need."

And on they talk until they would don helmets, saddle up, and roar away in first gear, the boldest among them shifting to second.

There is a rival bike gang in the area. Yong guys, mostly. Some of them have Harleys too, others cannot afford one and ride imports. But unlike the "Pro's" they do not have an official gang name. Many do not even have jobs or homes. They are young and full of real rebellion. Once there were rumors of a potential biker fight between the two factions. It was supposed to begin with a race to a predetermined area followed up by a fist fight, or as the "Pros" were calling the anticipated melee, a "rumble" The problem was that the young guys got tired of waiting for the "Pros'" to arrive, you see the "Pros" do not take their bikes out of second gear, or it seems so. They travel well under the speed limit. After a long wait the young guys went home. Good thing too, because I don't think those young bucks want to mess with guys that suffer from the Physical ailments that plague the "Pros".

Dod's most recent midlife crisis involved an SUV, a luxury SUV with computers, and navigation systems, and heated seats, and wipers for the headlights and a sun roof.

Now, most of us outdoorsmen in rural Pa have a 4X4 . Dod often insulted our treasured hunting vehicles. But, here he was in a luxury four-wheel drive himself. Dod proudly stepped out of his Yuppie tank. The guys and I were standing in my yard. It is worth noting that Dod and I used to be neighbors. He moved because we had very different opinions on lawn care. For instance, he mowed every three days, whether the grass needed it or not. And let's face it, how could it need to be cut in just three days? I, on the other hand, cut my yard every three weeks, sometimes. It isn't that I do not respect a well-groomed lawn, I certainly do. But...There are only so many hours in the day, and when work is done and I have a choice between mowing grass and running dogs...well...three weeks is as long as I have found that the grass can grow without being too much to handle. It's bad when you have to run the weed whacker to get the grass low enough to mow.   And even then I sometimes have to mow using all kinds of neat tricks like pushing the mower as if it were "riding a wheelie" in order to keep the mower from stalling in the jungle like grass.

Anyhow, the boys and me were standing on my shaggy lawn when Dod jumped out of his SUV, hiked up his pants by the side belt loops with a snort, and swaggered up to us

(So help me, he swaggered). He was, of course, dying for us to ask him about his new purchase.

"Wow! Hey Dod! Is that a new haircut?" Lenny asked.

"No," Dod answered, crestfallen at the fact that Lenny failed to ask about his Yuppie transport.

"Dod," I said, "Be careful you don't walk into that Ford pick-up truck th--". And right at that moment Dod bumped into the rusting heap (AKA F-250), buried under a thick luxurious lawn.

"OUCH!" Dod roared, "I just came to get some help with my vehicle."

"Can't do it," Lenny said.

"Why?"

"Because. No man can work on these new vehicles in a yard without computers. Why do you think we drive older vehicles?" Lenny answered.

"We drive them because we can find the damn spark plugs in them, that's why!" Eddie growled, "And we can adjust the idle."

"Yessir, I love carburetors." Lenny said, "And as far as I care they can keep those powered locks and powered windows and all of that stuff!"

And there we stood, in solidarity, as people who love to work on our own vehicles. Sometimes we even change parts that aren't worn out yet. Why? Because WE CAN! I sometimes change a fuel filter every 5,000 miles. I just do it because I can see the fuel filter. Not only that, but I don't have to drop the gas tank to do it.

"You know how long it takes to change the plugs in my wife's car?" Eddie asked. Dod shook his head in the negative, Eddie answered his own question "One hour and fifteen minutes! Fifteen minutes for the front three, and an hour for the back three!" Eddie opened up the hood on his old pick-up and began to tighten up some things, none of which were loose. "HA! HA HA." He gloated as nuts and bolts did just what he wanted.

"Remember the good old days when you just kept guessing until you found the root cause of a car's troubles?" Lenny reminisced

"Well, yes," Dod said, "But it cost more money by the time I paid the mechanic for all the trips."

"Mechanic?" Lenny snorted, "You don't get it. The whole point of a nice old four wheel drive is working on it yourself. It is cheaper to guess wrong on two or three parts than it is to pay for one computer diagnostic." Lenny dreamed into the days of yore when a set of sockets and wrenches could reach everything that you needed to fix, back before the days of specialty tools and extra specialty tools. Today, most car hoods won't even close if you leave a socket setting inside the motor--there isn't enough room left over in there to accommodate the socket and the hood latch.

"I just wanted to get a four wheel drive like you fellows have, only newer and better." Dod said. The guys looked him over.

"Where is your Harley?" Eddie asked.

"The Pros have started a new policy. Now we mostly just polish our bikes and drive to each other's houses in luxury SUV's to look at them."

"Say Dod," I said, "Your luxury SUV is sort of on the wrong side of town here. These are all woods hardened, seasoned, non-luxury hunting vehicles. We get them scratched. We haul firewood. What did you want to use that thing of yours for anyway?"

"I want the four wheel drive in case I have to take the grandkids to daycare, and it is raining." Dod said.

"You don't need four wheel drive for rain," Lenny said, "Is that thing posi-traction or limited slip or what?"

Dod answered with a blank stare, blinking occasionally.

"You don't even have enough ground clearance on that new vehicle of yours to get over a speed bump!" Eddie attacked, looking under the behemoth.

I could see it getting real ugly. Everyone was taking out their frustration on Dod. No one liked the state of automotive manufacturing, and Dod (and his luxury SUV) were taking the brunt of the frustration. "Guys," I said, "Let's just hear Dod out. He might need something that we can help him with."

Lenny rolled his eyes. "Fine. What is it?" He looked at Dod."

"I have some side rail steps I want to have welded onto the vehicle."

Eddie started laughing, "It isn't high enough off the ground to need them, Dod!"

"Lenny, I will make it worth your while, I promise." Dod said, "How about free dental exams for all your kids?"

Lenny thought for a second, scratching his chin. "That and one more thing," he demanded.

"Name it."

Lenny walked over and whispered something into Dod's ear. Dod nodded in agreement and they shook hands. "Follow me," Lenny said as he jumped into his truck and fired up the big V-8, "We will do this real quick at my garage. A little weld, a few bolts, and we will be done."

A few hours later I saw the SUV driving down the street, I happened to be mowing the yard with a sickle, trying not to dull the blade on metallic objects like axles and other objects hidden in the lawn. Dod slowed down as he creeped by, his new steps hovering a few inches off the road. The passenger side power window slowly lowered on the awkward Yuppie tank. As the tinted window receded into the door I saw Lenny with a big grin, looking right at me. He stuck his head out the window and said, "Nanny nanny boo boo, I can hunt where you do!" Darn Lenny. Now he had permission to hunt the pussy willow farm too. I yelled back at him, "Well so what! It doesn't take much of a dog to hunt a place so full of rabbits!" It was too late though. Dod was already roaring off, must have been running 60 miles per hour, grinning like a man who has never filled a gas tank on a big 4x4 when gas prices were this high.

POTLICKIN', HEADBANGIN', MEAT HUNTIN' HOBBY HOUNDS

Ah yes, I have potlickin', headbangin', meat huntin' hobby hounds. At various times, my hounds have been described in all of these aforementioned ways, even though some of those terms are contradictory. None of this ought to be unexpected in the world of beagling, where people get hypersensitive about their dogs. I dare say that you could insult most beaglers' wife and kids and get no reaction, but if you were to doubt the skills of their brag hound the gloves would come off and the sleeves would be rolled up.

No doubt these mutts of mine will lick a pot. Moreover, they will lick a plate, a pan, a saucer, a butter dish, a spoon, a ladle, a strainer, a mug, a glass, a casserole dish, a cookie pan, a children's sippy cup, an adult's goblet, a rolling pin, a roaster, a spatula, a whisk, tongs, and any other item that is left unattended with a bit of food odor on it. This, of course, is the cardinal sin of beagling for some people--keeping a dog as a pet. I once had a beagler tell me:

"You can't have them dogs in the house they won't hunt!"

"Really?" I responded, "Well, for God's sake don't tell the dogs because they have been hunting for years."

"Not in the cold, they will never be able to walk in the snow." He rebutted.

"They must be laying down in the snow then. Because when I let them out in the yard in the winter I can't get them to stop playing in the snow and come back in. And they seem to go hunting with me all winter too." I answered.

"Well, sure, but they can't hunt in subzero weather."
The criticism continued.

"You may be right sir, I no longer hunt until it gets up
to at least 20 degrees F. That is for my comfort, not the
dogs'. The dogs do well in that temperature, I just do not
enjoy hunting in subzero weather myself, and so I haven't
tested my hounds under those conditions recently." I
answered.

"Well, it takes an outdoor hound to do it." He grinned.

"Could be. I tell you what, the next time you go out
hunting in subzero weather, call me. I will go with you and
watch how good your beagles are. You only live a few miles
away, I can really be educated," I grinned back. Of course
he nodded and took my number. He never called to go
hunting, not in any temperature.

The truth of the matter is that a beagle can eat table
scraps and be a pet and still hunt very well. It is not,
however, easy to "Go for the gold" and "Be all you can be"
in the field trial sport if you keep just a few pets. It's
harder to get rid of a pet when it has a fault or two that
won't do. However, having said that, I have owned just as
many field champions as the vast majority of the field
trialers I associate with--ZERO. All of that complaining
about house dogs, all of that complaining about beagles
that don't live "in a pen where all they know is rabbits."
And those guys--most of them--have the same number of
FD CH dogs as me.

Shall we continue with headbanging? Oh my, do I have
headbangin' hounds. The term comes from the
presupposition that the dog is so fast that it doesn't stop or
turn until it bangs its head off a tree. In reality the term is
applied to any dog faster than somebody else's hound.
This, of course, is not hard to do in Western Pennsylvania.
I haven't done a statistical study, but it would not surprise
me if Western Pennsylvania had one of the highest
concentrations of brace clubs in the entire country.
Please, don't get me wrong, there are some gundoggers in
this part of the state as well. By and large the gundoggers
do not associate too freely with the brace boys. There are
exceptions however, where clubs will run a brace trial and
a gundog trial, (usually a gundog brace trial) and

sometimes you can't really tell much difference in the two licensed trials.

The problem arises when people read. You see, when you read the words "gundog" brace, you expect to see "gundogs," and consequently, people show up to run "gundogs." Obviously, they get disappointed. Many of these guys will go to the judges and complain, and will be told something to ease the anger of the fellow who drove all that way. Most people take the disappointment and go home. I once drove several hours to a trial where the dogs were walking the rabbit on a high scent morning with a gentle rain. As I left I heard an old timer remark "Get that headbanger out of here." I did not get upset at the comment, but it did make me curious because most of my friends pick on the same hound for running the middle or back of the pack. Of course their hounds don't walk a rabbit on a wet morning either.

Once a dog gets rabbit wise it can be useless for trials in many places. The dog gains skill and wisdom, and might lose a little style. In more stylish regions a hound without more style than accomplishment stands very little chance of placing. It sounds sinful, but it is true. I have actually talked to people who prefer to condition their hounds by "roading" them on a lead tied to a four wheeler rather than condition the dogs on rabbits because they are worried about the dog getting rabbit wise. When you see these guys around the brush pile, you can expect to get your hounds labeled as a headbanger.

Meat hounds. This is another favorite label floating around. More often than not this critique comes from the guy who has some really good dogs--but has forgotten about hunting. Let's face it--it does not take the best beagle to go out and shoot a rabbit. Because of that, many guys quit hunting. They claim that hunting rabbits doesn't do anything for them. That may be true, but I can't think of a hound I ever owned that didn't benefit from hunting.

"Oh, I imagine you have some good meat hounds, but that doesn't make a good beagle." My training pen friends will say.

"Well, no," I agree, "All good hunting beagles are not necessarily good trial hounds--but EVERY good field trial dog ought to be a good hunting dog." I always reply, "And the very fact that dogs are tested for gun shyness indicates that some entries, in fact, are not hunting dogs."

The part of this derogatory term "meat hound" that is hardest to explain is that sometimes the venom injected by the insult is given from gundoggers with more anger directed at the hunter than the walkie-talkie guys will hurl at the same hunting dogs. It is as if there is some sort of disdain from a few gundog field trialers for the hunter. God knows that there are slob hunters out there worthy of disdain, but the fact is that it is baffling that owners and breeders of gundogs will, at times, express this kind of disgust towards hunting.

It is as if these guys feel they have climbed into a new echelon of houndsmanship and it is a cut above the hunt. After all, it is the hunt that gives meaning to chase, and that is what gives meaning to our sport. I am sympathetic, however, as I would acknowledge whole-heartedly that the best hounds must be more than just good hunting dogs-- but there is no reason for these feelings to manifest themselves as they so often do in the form of insults towards the hunter and his hunting dog. Hey, it is the hunter that these guys call when a dog doesn't pan out for them, and it is the hunter that pays them the money for their started hounds that drop out of the trials and the hunter who buys the puppies.

All of the insults hurled at the gunning beagler come from behind the enclosed running grounds, where hounds run contained. Wow, have I seen some dogs pound inside the fences; running like a dream with amazing drive, great jump, and flawless check work. But some of those same dogs could hardly be found even with a tracking collar if they weren't tonguing. They do not handle and they do not obey. Ask the owner to go hunting and they panic--the dog has never really been broke from deer, because Fido has never had to run in an environment with many deer, and never outside of a fence.

I can hear some talking now, "Ford, you're full of it. Those are simply matters of training. All dogs can be broke from deer, all dogs can be trained to handle, and all dogs can be taught to follow the basics of obedience."

So show me. Finish the training of the hounds. It can't be that hard to do--regular 'ol hunters do it all the time with regular 'ol meat hounds.

And some of us do it with hobby hounds. It is an irony that a hound called "headbanger" by some people will be called "hobby hound" by others. More often than not this means a dog isn't fast enough or doesn't have enough endurance. Yet, as I think about this term, I think I can say that it is the most appropriate insult for the hounds I own. This is because hounds are, in fact, a hobby for me. I do, in fact, have a job outside of beagles. And beagles serve as a great pastime away from the stresses of work and life.

Most beaglers I associate with fall into a few categories. There is hobbyist like me who has many other engagements. We have the retired beagler, who does not have the burden of working for a living, and yet has a pension to play with the dogs. Some beaglers are self-employed and have the luxury of time. There is also the guy on welfare or disability who is too injured to work but is more than able to run after hounds day after day. He supplements his income with a litter of puppies now and again. Of all these groups, the most maligned is the guy who runs as a hobby, at least in some field trial settings.

No, I like the term hobby hound. I can handle that. Beagling is a wonderful hobby for most of us. We run our hounds when we get done working, or before we go to work. We look forward to the opening day of the season so that we can get out and do some hunting. We might join a club to run a bit, and we might go to some trials. But the reality is that it is one of those hobbies that gets into our blood and takes over. And I am as fond of the insults as anybody--the walkie-talkies and the potlickers and the headbangers, and the meat hounds, and the stylists, and all the rest. It is the way that we separate our dogs from somebody else's dogs.

So, be sure to get out in the brush and say hello this fall. I'll be outside the fence, where I am almost always to be found. I should have some potlickin', headbangin', meat huntin' hobby hounds with me, and I look forward to seeing you in the field--only don't look for me at subzero

temperatures--this is just a hobby to me, albeit an all
consuming one.

SMALL GAMES OF CHANCE, GRAND EXITS, AND OTHER METHODIST NO-NO'S

Palm Sunday was eventful this year. It is a prominent feature on the liturgical calendar for most churches, and the significance of Christ entering Jerusalem is an obviously important event for Christians. But this Palm Sunday was eventful for a more mundane reason.

I was preaching about Jesus sending a disciple to get the brand-new colt. I was emphasizing the way that Christ makes us willing and cheerful givers of our gifts and talents and so forth. I contrasted this kind of giving with the kind of giving that we can do for wrong reasons or with wrong intentions. For instance, I never mail my IRS payment in until April 15th. They can wait to get their money--I am not giving willingly. On the topic of giving, I also mentioned an event from some time ago when I was not leading worship in our two little churches because the children were leading us. I sat with the congregation.

I mentioned how I gave my tithe to the first worship service. When I arrived at the second service the kids led the entire service and I merely had to enjoy the music and the fun that the children were giving to us older folks. I sat in the pews. And in that Palm Sunday sermon I commented that I got nervous when the plate came by because I was afraid that people--unaware that I had already tithed an hour earlier--would think that I was "A cheap pastor" if I didn't put something in the plate. After all, how would they know that I donated earlier in the morning?

Now, "cheap pastor" is not a disturbing phrase. But let us keep in mind that I said this phrase in a United Methodist Church. There are three phenomena that

happen every Sunday in United Methodist Churches.
First, you can rest assured that there will be many in
attendance who are *bona fide* Octogenarians (80 years of
age or older). The second phenomenon is that many of
these faithful Methodists will be hard of hearing. And
lastly, you can rest assured those whose hearing is most
impaired will sit as far to the back of the sanctuary as they
can possibly sit. Many will arrive at church an hour early
to ensure their spot in the back. Their motto is, "I must be
in the back row."

Let's go back to the phrase "Cheap Pastor." It is not a
phrase that is heard very often. But it rhymes with a very
common phrase, a phrase that can be heard daily, albeit in
settings other than church--"Cheap bastard." I am told
that Many people gasped, and some had their jaws hang
open as if they had just witnessed a tragic car wreck. I
guess from a preaching stand-point, the consensus was
that it appeared more like a train wreck. I was oblivious to
the misperception. Half of the congregation heard the
phrase "Cheap pastor" which is in fact what I said. The
other half heard me cussing in the pulpit.

It was days before I realized what was being talked
about, and it was weeks before the whole mess was sorted
out. Those with better hearing helped explain to those who
are hearing impaired. It was a reverse Freudian slip--a slip
of the ear rather than the tongue. Granted I have said the
word bastard before, and worse, but not in church. Now,
what does any of this have to do with beagles? It has to
do with field trials. There are certain expectations that
are placed upon clergy. Not swearing from the pulpit
would be one of them. But there are others that I am sure
you could name with ease. In truth, they are expectations
that we should all have of everyone.

There is one social refrain that is particular to United
Methodists, and a few other denominations--an expectation
to not gamble. Our denomination is very clear on this
issue. The reasoning being that the people who get
addicted to gambling are those who can least afford it.
This means no lotto tickets, no bingo, no poker runs, no
raffles, and no fifty-fifty tickets. Ironically, there seems to
be no prohibition against the stock market, which is where

the church gambles with my retirement--I mean invests my pension.

Don't get me wrong. I am not pro-gambling by any means. I figure casinos and such are making money or they wouldn't be in business. The odds are against winning, and I agree with my denomination's stance. But there are charities and groups that I would like to support--beagle clubs, for instance. Clubs routinely raffle off a bag of dog food (usually a brand that I do not feed my hounds) or a fifty-fifty, or some other item to help raise money. I used to try to explain my position.

"No thank you," I would say, "I would not like to buy a raffle ticket. But can I make a donation and then the club can keep the money I donate?"

"No."

"Why not? Can't I just donate some money--" I started

"You have to buy a ticket to donate."

"I can't."

"Why not?" the guy asked.

"It is against my religion." That answer usually stymies a lot of people. After all, many churches have small games of chance as part of their weekly functions. I have no problems with other churches doing this, and I have to explain that my denomination forbids it.

"Whaddya mean it is against your religion?" he asked, holding the raffle tickets.

"I am forbidden to gamble in any way."

"What are you a Buddhist?"

"No." I shook my head.

"Do you belong to a cult?"

"No."

"Vegetarian?"

"Not hardly." I said, "I love meat."

"Well, then what are you?"

"Methodist." I confessed

"Me too. Buy a stupid ticket..."

Imagine my surprise when I took a pastor friend's little kid to a field trial one Saturday, and he bought a gazillion raffle tickets with the five dollars that I gave him to buy trinkets and junk and soda pop. Apparently the raffle ticket seller felt that the kid was picking them up for me

and sold them to the kid. He won too. I looked sheepish
when I took the kid home and he walked up to his folks--
Methodist pastors as well, and the child said, "Mommy!
Look I won something at the trial!"

Mom turned looking for a trophy or a ribbon and saw
her kid's toothy grin lugging in a bag of dog food, "This is
great!" the kid yelled, "All I had to do was buy these
tickets..." On a good note, I haven't been asked to baby-sit
for them again. His parents are afraid that I will move him
on to hard liquor and tobacco products next. Maybe even
usury or building idols.

Being a pastor also prevents me from doing the grand
exit. The grand exit is what I call it when anyone leaves a
trial with wheels spinning and gravel flying because their
hound either did not win or did not place or did not make
second series. The grand exit can be an awesome display
of dejection. It can also be a bit harrowing if the driver is
not able to control a slide as he (and it is always a man, I
have never seen a woman beagler do this) sidewinds down
the dirt road. There is nothing quite as amusing as a
grand exit that ends in a ditch and requires another
beagler to extricate the stuck vehicle. It is a dangerous
thing though, and for this reason I always stake my
hounds out near the protection of my own vehicle,
ensuring sure that no one can run them over. It just
wouldn't look right for a pastor to do the Grand Exit. I
have come close to being run over by devout Christians as
they leave, though. I once took cover in the bushes as a
pick-up truck came sliding at me after second series was
announced. The truck had a front license plate that read
"Co-Pilot: Jesus." I was hoping that the Lord would move
from co-pilot to main pilot as that truck zeroed in on me.
No, I won't be doing the Grand Exit, even under the worst
disappointment

I have had some disappointments this year too. I had a
dog come back for second series in a trial and measure
out. I had a hound back into winners' pack after some
other poor beagler's hound measured out and then got
picked up sixth (and probably should have been picked up
seventh! The judges were right to yank him out of there). I
had one judge tell me that my bitch "Didn't do anything

wrong, and had a whole bunch of score for checks, but didn't have any points on the straight-aways." I looked through the rulebook for the term "straightaway" but haven't found it yet.

But no matter how disappointed I might be I take my potlickers home with a smile and a thank you, even if I feel disappointed. Those are the breaks of trials. Nope, I will never do a hole-shot pulling out. I hope to see you all at the trials with my potlickers. Maybe we can sit back and tell a few stories. I don't even try to explain why I don't buy raffle tickets anymore. But I will support the clubs by putting extra money in the coffer for coffee refills. My denomination hasn't criticized my caffeine addiction...yet. I always throw in a little extra for those refills to support the club. So if you see a fellow who doesn't buy your tickets when you come by me, please understand that it is a rule I have to follow. Please don't think of me as a cheap Pastor.

FEBRUARY SNOW

February is about when our snow starts some years. Of course we get snow before that, but in recent years it never seems to hang on all winter like it did. It seems like we receive series of snows and thaws all through the winter. It is like watching a bad offense in football, except in this case it is winter that seems to be guilty of repeated "false starts." My memory may be subject to a romantic desire for snow wherein nostalgia mistakenly inserts wintry blasts that did not exist into my childhood, but I remember winter being more substantial as a kid—colder winters with the snow plowed into mountains at the edges of parking lots. Winter seemed formidable—and not just for the young. I remember snow tires on everyone's cars. I am not talking about the tires that are labeled as winter tires now. I mean the ones that had massive steel studs that slapped at the snow and road with bad intentions. There were always chains for the tires as well; they always sat next to the jumper cables in the trunk, waiting for the time to be marshaled into service. The jumper cables and tire chains were used semi-regularly and were as commonplace as an ice scraper. I still remember the rear wheel drive cars and people having to drive home backwards up the steeper hills when the snow was falling hard. And the snow stayed on the ground and did not melt until spring. I recall one particularly fun winter when the snow of those plow-made snow banks hung on until the end of April, or at least the last tiny ice cube sized remnant made it until trout season opened in mid-April. We would ride the school bus and when we made our final approach to the school we would drive through caverns of frozen snow that were built by the plows.

Kids couldn't wait play outside at recess and in gym class, finally free from basketball in the gymnasium. The winter kept us inside doing calisthenics, wrestling, and basketball. Basketball was my least favorite and the longest lasting sport of the winter. The gym teacher feared wrestling because it quickly devolved into blood sport with no love and less rules. Basketball was the default sport of winter, and it was my least favorite because it seemed a bit artificial in the rules—the same exact event would be randomly called either an offensive or a defensive foul without rhyme or reason, based totally on whim it seemed, regardless of whose feet were or were not moving when contact occurred. I could not wait to emerge from basketball into the outside. Don't get me wrong, you could still see your breath in the air in some of those physical education classes, but the outside air was suitable for exercise. As long as you kept moving your toes would not go numb. The lawn would be green in late March, but the air chilly. Those caverns of plowed snow clung to winter so as to make you wonder if spring really was coming. They towered as guardians, sentinels of the cold, looking at us as if to say, "Don't get used to this warm weather. We got some air coming from the north of Canada."

I have only used my snowshoes once in the last few years, at least in Pennsylvania. Oh, I know I could go up towards Erie and find a deep band of keystone state flurries, but I do not hunt rabbits there, or at least I haven't in some years. I have no contacts there anymore. We get the snow in the Laurel Highlands too, albeit less. I merely lament the loss of persistent snow where I am. I am not trying to start a fight about snow and who gets more or who gets the most. I once talked to a fellow from Tug Hill at a field trial, and he was ready to fight every man in the room to defend his honor as the person who lives in the snowiest of all places. Good grief, it was as if his manhood was tied to snow.

No, what I miss is those winters where all of Northern and Western Pennsylvania would get that new dusting every night (or at least every couple nights). When I say dusting I mean 1-3 inches. Anymore the meteorologists carry on about three inches as if it were the same storm that doomed the Donner expedition. Three inches is a nice, thick dusting. We would get these small, regular, persistent snows and it didn't melt. You had a couple feet of accumulation in no time. 50+ degrees was not a common December event.

My snowshoes are only used out of state for the most part, or in an occasional drift in Pa. But it is February as you read this, and I am hopeful for snow. I remember last winter we got a bunch of lake effect snow in February. The weatherman said it was because the cold air was coming and Lake Erie wasn't frozen at all, as it might typically be. I can only hunt a few days in February in my home state. But I love to go out into the snow and walk through the Laurel and sneak though the pine and hemlock. I go out there looking for rabbit tracks.

In particular I like to look for places with more rabbit tracks than deer tracks. I haven't had much trouble with deer running hounds, but I try to place my hounds in rabbit rich environments. I have one prize bitch that is good about not starting a deer chase—but if another dog starts one she will surely finish it and look good! February is my time to scout for new places. I found a nice spot a few years ago on state game lands, which was a pleasant surprise because the state game lands can often be game-less. Much of the game lands are piles of shale that once held trees and bushes and weeds. I know the game commission is working on this land, but it takes time to reclaim a strip mine void of good topsoil. Last February I found a great concentration of rabbit tracks in late February when the rabbit population was at its annual low. This past fall I went to that honey hole many times for a hunt.

Snow always makes my dogs look good too. They are sight hunters in the drifts. They stick their noses in the tracks looking for the freshest scent and then they are off! Even my mutts can run check-free in fresh powder! Granted I am not as eager to run out in that subzero air as I was in my youth, but a nice 20 degrees day and a fine hound doing a good job in that crisp air on the fresh snow is heaven to me. The cold air seems to let the dog's voice bounce louder and cleaner through the hills and valleys. If it is a perfect day then the sun is bright, or maybe just a bit overcast, and the wind is calm allowing me to hear the hounds run. Maybe if I am at the edge of a farm I can smell the fireplace burning. That deep snow is the perfect answer to any fool who thinks that a fast dog is the wrong dog. You put a hound with more style than accomplishment down in the deeper snow and you might wait all day to see a rabbit. A hound with guts and go and giddy-up is sheer poetry in the deep snow.

I know people who won't even hunt rabbit until there is snow. That is a luxury I can't afford in Pa. It is January as I write this column. I have been hunting the second season here in warm air. It was 60 degrees one day, not at all as I remember winter. Yes, I know that the Rockies and parts of New England and other places have been hammered with the snow. Even so, I bet New England would have preferred that big ice storm to have arrived in colder air as snow and left the power running and the trees standing after it had passed. I have a few elderly parishioners who pray that we receive no snow; and some who even leave to avoid it all together, following the birds to Florida. I haven't the heart to tell them that I pray for MORE snow.

I get that same feeling when a storm is coming that I did as a child. Whenever a foot or more of snow would be forecast in my youth I always woke up early to hope for a two-hour delay from school or maybe even a cancellation if the storm was big enough. Spring will be here soon. I like winter to go out with gusto and a few snowflakes. I have my snowshoes ready, and the dogs are fit—all this bare ground has allowed them plenty of hard running chases. A fresh two inches every night would be great, not enough to be a problem, but a great powder to hunt. After all, there are only nine days to hunt rabbits in Pennsylvania before the season ends. Yes, just a few inches each night would be perfect. And then I will take a week's vacation to hunt hare north of here.

Don't tell my older parishioners, but that last bit was a prayer. They wouldn't be mad at me though if they knew the prayers that their great grand kids were saying. Those kids are asking for snow in much larger quantities. They probably don't like basketball.

HOUNDSMAN OR SPORTSMAN?

Maybe some of you have the same problem that I do—you friends make repeated accusations that you are not really a sportsman, but rather you are a guy who runs around the woods with dogs and spends way too much time and energy (and perhaps money) to shoot not so many pounds of meat (as compared to the bounty of a single deer) in the form of rabbits and hare. I don't think this makes us non-sportsmen, instead it seems that it simply solidifies our status as houndsmen. Houndsmen are a vanishing thing in a world of pavement, malls and crowded neighborhoods that are not in favor of barking hounds. Maybe you are wondering if you are more of a houndsman or sportsman, and if you are I have provided a test that is by no means scientific. I have begun with the assumption that I am a houndsman more than I am a sportsman; and I will test your outdoor practices to see if they agree with mine.

Let us start with spring turkey season which has ended by the time you read this. Do you hunt turkey with beagling clothes? All of my camouflage hats have the names of dog food companies or beagle clubs on them. This generates great amusement amongst my friends who wonder if I am really aware of what turkey hunting is supposed to look like. They all have face paint and grease on as if we are going to war in a jungle, I have a *Purina* hat with a green face net for bugs. Ha, you should see them double over in laughter when I bring a side by side 12 gauge with me. "What in the world is that?" they ask.

"My turkey gun, why?" I reply

"Bit small, ain't it"

"12 guage isn't enough?"

"Well, we got us a 12 gauge just for turkey—3 ½" shells."

"Hmm. Well, this gun of mine hardly ever gets used. I like my 16 gauge *fox*, but I use this monster for places where pheasant are known to roam during rabbit season and also for road trips. When I go out of state I hate to run out of ammunition and the 2 ½" shells that my fox use are hard to find. The 12 gauge *Stevens* is my road trip gun if I am hunting for a long time away from home. The 2 ¾" shells are easy to find anywhere."

"You use 2 ½" shells and 2 ¾" shells? I only use 3" for small game and 3 ½" for Turkey!" my friend says as he holds out his turkey gun. He looks at my 12 gauge *Stevens* with disdain. "That thing is made from wood and has no camo! You need a new 12 gauge!"

Well, I will tell you this," I answer, "I would love to own an *Ithaca* side by side of any kind, but especially a 12 gauge, no one seems to have one for sale. I think a rabbit hunter can appreciate such a gun the best. I held one once, much lighter than my *Stevens*." This usually ends the discussion about my qualifications as a turkey hunter. I always wait until lunch to explain that my turkey hunting boots were purchased for chasing hounds through tall, wet grass; and that they just happen to have a camouflage pattern on them by accident. That sends them over the edge.

Fishing season is no better. Some of my more devout fishing partners have carrying cases for their rods and racks in the truck for secure transportation. I tear my pole apart and place it in the storage bin on my diamond plate dog carrier. I put live bait in a container that goes in the same location. This is minor in comparison to my insistence that we fish after I run hounds in the morning. This makes no sense to any fisherman—but unless you are fishing for native trout it does not really matter—the stocked trout are virtually aquarium fish! Bass season is even more perplexing to my friends. I fish in a location where the dogs can chase rabbits while I am casting. If I have a concern for the beagles, I abandon the fishing and come back later. I caught the biggest bass of the year that way. I had left the rod attached to a makeshift clamp on the shore to retrieve a pair of beagles that were chasing hard in the general direction of a road. When I returned with the dogs I gave them water and leashed them to a shade tree. I picked up my rod and had the biggest bass that any of us caught that year. Apparently a floating jointed minnow that looks dead is as appealing as one that is being worked to look alive! If you use bass season to condition hounds, then you may be more of a houndsman than an outdoorsman.

Moving through the year, we arrive at Fall turkey season. I have become quite a success at this sport, which I will explain shortly. I know true blue turkey hunters that wear cammo and the minimum orange allowed by law and they do o.k. If I expect to see turkey in one of my rabbit hunting locations I take the 12 gauge (the *Stevens*). It is now legal to hunt turkey with dogs in PA during the fall. I own a beagle that loves to chase birds—sparrows in the yard, and anything from woodcock to grouse and pheasant in the woods. Sometimes when we are rabbit hunting he picks up on a bird and away he goes! Most of the birds flush long and I can't shoot. But I kill more birds than you might think with a beagle. All I know is turkey must really smell strong, because that dog will run the big birds like a demon. The things will circle too. In case you were wondering, lead a turkey about the same as a rabbit. Aim a little high on the follow up shot as they will try to fly. I recommend using the tighter barrel if you are using a side by side. I do all this while wearing an orange vest and an orange hat. Now, if your turkey season is a thing that only occurs if your beagles happen to rouse a bird, then it is clear that you are leaning more towards houndsman than sportsman.

Archery hunting is a rarity for me because it interferes with rabbit hunting. I suppose I do archery hunt a tad-bit, but everyone laughs because all my hunting clothes have dog hair on them. I tend to waste my time in the tree stand looking at potential brush piles for rabbits. The rifle season for deer is another matter. Are you the kind of hunter that hunts deer for the sake of the deer? Or do you manage rabbit habitat? I even deer hunt with rabbit hunting intentions. I always deer hunt—especially when filling my doe tags—in places where I train beagles. I have not had much trouble with deer running hounds in recent years, but I am a firm believer in running where there are more rabbits than deer. A scarcity of bunnies is a major problem when training, and I do not train or hunt in places where the rabbits are few and the deer are plenty. I even invite friends to come fill deer tags where I hunt rabbits. Heck, I even drive the woods for them. "Stay right here," I say, "Those pines always have deer in them. If the dog chases a rabbit in there a whole herd runs out before the beagle and rabbit emerge. You will want to look down the left edge of the tree line, and they will probably run right towards you." I walk into the brush and follow a path into the pines that the rabbits typically run, and very often a rifle shot is heard in short order. I then volunteer to drag the deer into the open field, where the rabbits seldom go, and field dress the deer. The crows find the gut pile faster, making quick work of it, and the beagles never have to encounter the mess in the second rabbit season.

So, it seems that I am a houndsman, a beagler, a chaser of the loveable breed first, and a sportsman second. Oh well, don't tell the experts, but my freezer isn't empty. I get trout, venison, turkey, pheasant, grouse, and woodcock as much as the next guy. Not to mention the rabbits. I have been chasing theses beagles since I was a little kid. My father always felt that a kid in the woods with beagles until after dark was safer than a son in town with the influence of other rambunctious teenage boys at any hour. Maybe he was on to something, even if it did turn out that my life has gone to the dogs and all my other outdoor hobbies are pursued with beagling equipment and rabbit management goals. I think, if he were alive, he would be pleased to know that you can now shoot turkey in front of dogs legally in Pennsylvania. Come to think of it, as I remember Thanksgiving dinners with wild turkey on the table, it seems to me that maybe he wasn't too worried about that law, he always shot a turkey over beagles.. To all you dads who take your kids to the woods with beagles —it makes a big difference—and Happy Father's Day.

Hunting with Howard

Not long ago, just before the start of hunting season, some fellows and I went tailgating. Not the kind with football and food, rather it was the kind where you drive way back into the old strip mines and let the hounds run while you drink coffee from thermoses and munch on various snacks that might be sitting in your vehicles.

The thermoses became necessary after no two people could decide on how to make coffee from a percolator pot on an open fire. Using the open fire and the pot sounded rustic and nature-like. A campfire is always nice to have around too. But there were constant complaints about the coffee--too strong for one, not strong enough for another. One fellow wanted flavored creamers, another wanted sugar substitutes. One guy would only drink decaf. So, after much discussion we decided to keep the fire, but each could bring the coffee of his choice. Shortly thereafter the fire faded away too. There was too much disagreement about how to get the fire started and even more debate about how to put the fire out. Trying to get beaglers to be civil can be an uphill battle.

But, one thing we all could agree upon is that folks are forever enjoying a good conversation that insults another man's job.

"You got it pretty good," Steve told me one sunny day, "You only work one day a week. Gives you all kinds of time to run dogs and go to any trial you want."

"That's right, Steve," I responded, "Actually I only work a half day each week. I am done by noon on Sundays. That's because I make so much money that I need the rest of the week to spend it all. Why you oughta go into the ministry."

"Don't you feel bad taking a paycheck from folks who donate the money in a plate to pay for it?" Ron chimed in.

"Not really. You work for the state, do you feel bad receiving a paycheck from taxes that were taken rather than donated?"

Ron laughed, "Well I guess I never saw it that way, but you can make those Friday or Monday trials easier than many of us can."

"That is true. I could, and on occasion I have. But I have missed out on lots of Sunday trials. And I have wanted to trial my 15" bitch lots of times and couldn't because the class always seems to run on Sunday." I answered.

"Maybe next year you could send your dogs out with Howard." Everyone had a good laugh. Everybody likes picking on Howard, especially when he isn't around, but no one seems to have much trouble giving him an earful in person either.

"What's so funny?" Steve asked.

"Ah nothing."

"What? What?"

"Howard's disabled, you know?"

"No sir, his legs work fine. I saw him run down a whole pack of dogs yesterday..."

"He ain't that kind of disabled."

"Well, his arms and shoulders are o.k. He was just stretching fence on his running grounds..."

"He ain't that kind of disabled either."

"But Howard's back seems real good. He was splitting firewood this past fall. Knotty twisted stuff that was donated to him for free. He moved right through it..."

"He ain't that kind of disabled neither none." Fred spit a stream of snuff juice.

"Well, what kind of disabled is he if his arms, legs and back work?"

"The kind of disabled that doesn't want to work!" Lenny shouted.

"He has cards that say he is a professional beagler. I could do that too if I didn't have to work. And got a check in the mail every month!" Ron seconded.

Steve spoke up, "Anyone ever hunt with Howard? He must have real good dogs. If he has all that time. Plus he has that fenced in pen of his. Almost a hundred acres, I hear."

I almost drown on my coffee. I then explained to Steve about the time Howard and I went hunting. Howard was pressing me to breed my bitch to his male. He had quite a bit of success with the dog in some gundog trials. Howard always teased me about my pets that lived in the house. He said you can't pet or play with a dog or it won't hunt rabbits. Then he wanted me to breed to his good gundog field trial hound.......

"Maybe Howard, maybe I will use that stud dog of yours. What say we go hunting with him first and see what we got there?" I suggested.

Beads of sweat bubbled up on Howard's forehead. "Sure," Howard said, come by my place and you can see him run."

"I'd like to see him hunt rabbits too." I added

"Ok....umm...bring a gun too, we can shoot a few off my land. It is rabbit season," Howard squeaked.

Howard and I ran inside of his professional running grounds. His hounds are some serious jump dogs. They roar into the brush and are quite eager to find a rabbit. Before too long the stud dog and the other hound with him were out of sight, turning only when they hit a tree or a fence. A faint bark poured down the hill to us. The dogs had a rabbit up and running, but they were almost out of ear shot. Up the hill we went. Howard and I climbed up and got in place to see the chase. The rabbit came out into the open and I pulled up my shotgun. "Wait!" Howard yelled, "The dogs are too close!"

I looked and expected to see a dog running mute on a sight chase, or maybe a real tight mouthed dog in the area. The rabbit hopped away. The beagles tongued in the brush, fifty yards behind the rabbit, working out a check. "What are you talking about Howard?"

"You can't shoot that close to the dogs. It makes them gun-shy."

"How do you figure?"

"Well, I have killed a lot of rabbits with that dog in there, but it is called gun-shy by some folks, and was made that way. You see, one time a guy fired over him at a trial and then he got picked up. Now the dog thinks that it is going to get picked up after a shot. And another time the blank gun was fired too close."

"Too close?"

"Yes. They shouldn't fire when they are close to the dogs. It is too loud!" Howard was shaking with anger.

"Well Howard, that blank gun is quieter at twenty yards than my 12 gauge is at forty yards. I think the dog is gun-shy. How far back you want them dogs when I shoot, Howard?"

"Oh, eighty or a hundred yards oughta be o.k."

Sometimes I shoot scared rabbits that far in front. But that isn't always the case. And in that pen of Howard's it would be impossible. There were way too many rabbits that have been run way too many times to be that scared. "Howard, I gotta tell ya. I really like the way your dogs pound a rabbit. But I don't know if I can hunt with a gun-shy dog, and I don't know if your dog handles well enough for me to use. I like a dog to hunt with me. What do you say we go out into the old coal strippings and get a wild rabbit?"

"Uh. You mean outside of a fence?"

"Well yes. The coal companies didn't plant fences when they reclaimed the land, just briars and bushes and evergreens. Don't worry, I am paranoid about roads, and I do not go anywhere near busy highways."

"Maybe. Say, why don't you shoot one in here however you want."

I did. And the stud dog ran like a scared rabbit. He came back in about ten minutes. "See," Howard started, "He ain't so much gun-shy as he is noise sensitive."

"Oh. O.k. I will have to remember that term."

"He was made that way! You can't shoot blank guns twenty and thirty yards from a dog and expect it to act right!" Howard was spraying the woods with saliva and his eyes were starting to glaze.

"I'm real sorry, but don't tell the bird hunters. They shoot a few steps away from their pointing dogs all the time. They haven't been told that it makes them gun-shy." I answered. "Maybe I will breed to this dog. I think you can fix gun-shy to some degree, but I just don't like they way this hound handles.

"Come here boy! Howard yelled, and the dog didn't come HERE! TALLY-HO!" Howard continued yelling 'Tally-ho' trying to get his dog to come. I tried to explain to him that I can't hunt with a dog that won't handle. And I would be embarrassed to have to yell tally-ho to get my dog to mind me."

"Fine. Let's go to your blasted coal mines!" Howard yelled, "Bring one of your dogs too!"

We dropped tailgates that same evening. It was early in hunting season, and the late afternoon sun was setting. We wouldn't have much time. I let my little male dog out and he hit the ground whining and whimpering with excitement. "Get in there," I said to the dog and it crawled into a brush pile with tail wagging. "Through here," I said and guided the dog down a gully and let him range out. We walked through some thick stuff and the dog roamed near me, nosing into a patch of briars here, and some wild grapes there.

"Not real enthusiastic, is he?" Howard flecked some saliva.

"No. He isn't the hardest hitting dog in the world. A big deer jumped up and ran. The dog stuck his nose in the air and smelled the high scent, and then, as if remembering being punished for that odor, Put his nose back lower and worked into some thickets. Two more deer jumped up well off to our right hand side. "I do like the way your dogs plow into the brush Howard. But this little hound of mine will get a rabbit going too."

"Lots of deer here," Howard noted, as he watched them bolt up a hill. The hound barked and a run was up. A circle and a half later the rabbit was shot. The dog was forty yards away.

"I have my own method for stopping gun-shyness," I told Howard, "My dogs are all housebroke. So I send them to houses with noisy kids. The kids like the dogs, and the beagles get used to noise. Nothing makes noise quite so well as kids." I worked the dog back towards the truck. "Down," I said, and the dog went to its belly. I picked him up and put him in the truck.

"That is what I would like to see my dogs do," I said, "But I will be honest, Howard. I like your dog's guts and drive and he still has line control. I wouldn't mind seeing my dogs do more of that. And God knows I don't have any field trial success like you do."

Howard dropped the tailgate and let his stud dog out. It ran straight until it hit a scrub oak tree and then turned, until it slammed up against an old coal slag pile, and turned again. I couldn't see it anymore, but it barked and back came the chase a bit later. The first time the rabbit came by it was just a blur through a tiny opening. No one could get a shot. That dog stayed true and brought the little rodent back again, this time into a bigger clearing. One shot dropped the rabbit. The dog was way back in the brush and didn't flinch.

We couldn't catch the dog to go home. We tried "Tally-ho." I tried "Come Here," a phrase that I have always had success using. I let out a loud whistle, which also works well for me. Howard even barked like a dog to try and get the dog to hark into him. Every once in a while we would see the dog flash by in the brush, looking for a rabbit, but not chasing one at that time, turning whenever it bumped into a tree or rock.

The day was saying goodbye to the last ray of sunlight when the stud dog flew by on a monster buck--and not a buck rabbit. The poor dog never had to run in an area that had many deer. Howard was yelling "Tally-Ho!" at the top of his lungs, chasing the hound to get it. I told Howard that I would go home and put my dog away and get some flashlights...

..."And that is the story of hunting rabbits with Howard." I told Steve. "But he doesn't have to get a job, and he sells some pups and earns money on a few stud fees. And when the rabbit population is low and you and and the rest of us are scratching to get a good run, Howard still can turn his hounds out in his pen."

"Did he ever get his dog back that night?" Steve asked
"Sure did." I answered.
"How?"

"I heard that dog pounding that deer hard. I had been looking for the dog for awhile. I turned off my flashlight and hid in the brush and waited for the dog to come by."

"Are you telling me you caught that dog, in the dark, driving a deer at full cry? I don't believe you. That must be one of those pastor-lies."

"Not a lie. I caught the dog. I waited until that deer crashed by me and I moved over to the area. And when that dog was ten yards away I fired both barrels of my twelve gauge high brass into the air at once. Dog stopped on a dime. It started to run the other way, but then I hit him right between the eyes with my flashlight. The Bright light kept him still long enough to catch him."

"Well, that was nice of you to help Howard catch the dog." Steve mused.

"Yeah, but now his dog is afraid of bright lights. Howard won't call it 'light-shyness' though. He says the dog is 'light sensitive.' "

CPSIA information can be obtained at www.ICGtesting.com
Printed in the USA
BVOW02s1906121214

379216BV00008B/457/P